Upsizing Democracy:

Confronting the Right Wing Assault on Government

Lee Cokorinos, Democracy Strategies

Published by In the Public Interest

Also by Lee Cokorinos

Infrastructure Privatization in the New Millennium
The Oxford Handbook of State and Local Government Finance
(with Ellen Dannin)

Target San Diego
Conservative think tank efforts to build policy influence
and political power in greater metropolitan areas.

The Assault on Diversity:
An Organized Challenge to Racial and Gender Justice
How conservative organizations have waged a legal and
political campaign against affirmative action and other
social justice initiatives.

Copyright © 2007 Lee Cokorinos
In the Public Interest
All rights reserved.
ISBN: 1532912234
ISBN-13: 9781532912238

Table of Contents

Foreword

"Organize discontent – that is our strategy."
Howard Phillips, Founder, Conservative Caucus, 1979

"Good organizations don't just happen. They take root in a body of shared beliefs. They flow from strong leadership with vision, initiative and determination to reach great goals."
President Ronald Reagan, 1981 addressing the NRA

"What is power? It is the ability to tell others what the issues are, what the issues mean, and identify who the good guys and bad guys are. That is power."
Howard Phillips, Conservative Caucus, early 1980s

For decades conservative theorists and politicians aligned with and funded by corporate interests have employed a sophisticated strategy to accomplish a simple objective: Convince the American public that government is "the problem" in the hopes of shrinking government until it is so ineffective that it can be "drown[ed] in a bathtub." They have enjoyed tremendous success. In 1958, 73 percent of Americans said they had faith in the federal government; today public trust in government stands at just 26 percent – a historic low.

If the public does not believe government can do anything right, progressives cannot prevail in the many significant policy battles in which we are engaged. If government is deemed incompetent, surely it cannot guarantee quality, affordable health care for all. If government is considered wasteful and inefficient, it cannot be trusted to raise revenue and invest it wisely. If government regulations are intuitively seen as overly burdensome, it becomes all the harder to safeguard the environment, protect consumers and strengthen workers' rights.

Lee Cokorinos has written a coherent and insightful history of the ideas, people, institutions and strategies of an increasingly capable and aligned conservative infrastructure. It is an invaluable read for those of us who strive to reconnect the American people with the value of public solutions and the need to create accountable, responsive and inclusive governments that work for the many and not just the few.

Donald Cohen
Executive Director, In the Public Interest

I. Introduction:

"For too many of us the political equality we once had won was meaningless in the face of economic inequality. A small group had concentrated into their own hands an almost complete control over other people's property, other people's money, other people's labor — other people's lives. (…) Against economic tyranny such as this, the American citizen could appeal only to the organized power of Government."

> --Franklin Delano Roosevelt

The issue of competent, active and accountable government is back on the national agenda. After decades of ideological attacks, a series of recent events has undermined the conservative movement's basic message of downsizing and defunding government. The Federal government's failure to prevent the 911 terrorist attacks despite ample warning, the incessant private contracting scandals in Iraq and domestically, the disastrous response to Hurricane Katrina by a "streamlined" and "outsourced" FEMA,[1] the consequences of government inaction on market-generated global warming, and the bankruptcies and economic damage caused in part by weak financial regulation of Enron and WorldCom have brought some long missing balance back into the discussion.[2]

These and other events have also seriously tarnished the overblown rhetoric of "free market" efficiency long championed by libertarian ideologues and government contractors alike, which the right has used to denigrate the role of government and offered as an alternative through deregulation and privatization. The 2000-2001 California energy crisis, which was produced by corporate manipulation of electricity prices (which rose 670% over a thirteen month period), showed that eliminating government regulation may be a good bumper sticker slogan but that the "free market" can have dangerous financial consequences for working families and the effective functioning of the economy.[3]

Right wing politicians and ideologues have made a living for a generation by ridiculing what they see as the philosophically-rooted incompetence of liberalism and the welfare state. But they now find themselves trapped by their own governing record of massive pork barrel spending, enormous budget deficits, administrative failure, cronyism and lobbying scandals. Besides provoking public disgust and feeding cynicism about government, this spectacle has also produced an unprecedented level of ideological disarray and disunity in conservative ranks.[4]

Simplistic campaign sloganeering against excessive government, a dominant theme in American politics since the 1980 election produced a landslide victory for Ronald Reagan, is losing its edge as debates play out across the country on which specific programs are to be cut or funded. The conservative paradigm, rooted in ideology and profiteering rather than practical problem solving, may be running out of steam at this point. Major victories by citizen groups defending public funding of needed programs and services have been scored against right wing strategist Grover Norquist's cherished "Taxpayers' Bill of Rights" laws in Colorado and elsewhere.

Colorado business leaders are now warning their colleagues across the country not to drink the ideological snake oil of locking in unwise tax cuts and artificial ceilings. "TABOR is a proven failure in Colorado," they wrote in a letter to fellow businesses in Maine where a TABOR bill is under consideration. "We strongly encourage that you do not repeat Colorado's mistake."[5] Those who wish to "starve the beast" of government, as Reagan's budget director David Stockman said, or "drown government in the bathtub," as Norquist put it have a serious credibility problem and they know it.

Although the issue of running government effectively has sometimes been personalized and reduced to a question of President Bush's competence,[6] the right's failure to govern successfully is also rooted in its aversion to government itself and distaste for the openness and accountability necessary to make government work effectively. "This conservative presidency and Congress imploded, not despite their conservatism," political scientist Alan Wolfe writes, "but because of it."[7] The can-do authoritarianism of the right seems to have boiled down to authoritarianism without the can-do.

Just as importantly, the Midas-like compulsion of right wing lobbyists and activists to turn government services and contracting into cash for their corporate patrons has produced, as in the case of the Medicare drugs bill, the worst of all worlds—labyrinthine bureaucratic complexity, monopoly profit protections for pharmaceutical companies and a vastly more expensive program than could have been provided through a politically incorrect straight-up government agency.[8] The problem for the right is that this approach to governing is necessary for its very political survival, which is based on the successful coordination of corporate funding, conservative politicians and the right wing media and think tank infrastructure. It is a structural barrier that makes the right incapable of governing in the public interest at all levels of government.

<u>A Failed Model of Government</u>

Beyond the issue of incompetence, the right also faces a number of serious challenges to its longstanding domination of the terms of debate on the role of government at the national, state and local level. It has run out of workable substantive ideas on what government can do to confront the structural problems facing American society at each of these levels. The broad philosophical approach that has guided it for a generation simply does not provide a coherent model of good government or even of the effective use of market mechanisms to advance the public good.

The right is also now vulnerable on one of its traditional strong points, that it understands how the economy works and can craft policies to sustain growth and prosperity. If fifty years of New Deal governing philosophy foundered on the rocks of "stagflation" and "malaise" in the 1970s, the conservative movement faces a similar convergence of economic, social and political challenges to its vision of government's limited role. "Malaise makes a comeback," *The Boston Globe* recently declared. Stagflation, the combination of inflation and stagnation that conservatives used to kill off the Keynesian demand management model in the 1970s, is also now making a comeback in the headlines.[9]

Globally, under the stewardship of the right the U.S.' economic and financial position has steadily deteriorated. Massive levels of debt have been piled up to simultaneously finance militarism and consumerism. Deficit spending and corporate tax cutting has simply filled the coffers of transnational corporations who invest elsewhere, while domestic investment and employment softens or declines. The national debt ceiling has been raised to $9 trillion to avoid an unprecedented national default. A record $2.69 trillion in net debt to the rest of the world has been racked up, threatening a surge in interest rates, a weakening of the dollar and a contraction of the economy.[10] The U.S. now faces a $763 billion annual trade deficit, making the debt even more difficult to repay and contributing to the loss of nearly 3 million manufacturing jobs.[11]

Domestically, steeply rising healthcare costs and gas prices, unregulated "Big Box" store growth, suburban sprawl and a crisis in the supply of affordable housing are also becoming important issues around the country. New cross-class constituencies have been created to push for government action to promote shared prosperity, labor rights, contracting transparency and accountability, democratic planning and community empowerment. The right has taken notice of these new green shoots of a resurgent progressive politics and considers this trend a mortal threat to its political dominance.[12]

Major decisions on government's role in supporting public health, public services and social mobility (e.g., broad access to higher education, the cost of which has increased 57% at public universities since 2000) are on the horizon. As the GDP growth rate slides, it is becoming clearer that unchecked "market" forces are producing stagnant or declining living standards, heightened income inequality and a poorer quality of life for many Americans.[13] Poverty has increased every year that the Bush administration has been in power. This picture cuts against the basic philosophical and electoral message of the conservative movement: that unregulated capitalism and a minimal state bring prosperity, social advancement and freedom.

Economic problems that contributed in the late 1970s and early 1980s to the triumph of "supply side economics,"[14] such as inflationary pressures, rising global interest rates, destructive competition, declining real investment and a weakening U.S. currency are now mounting up on the right's watch.[15] Discussion of an expanded role for government in directly regulating financial markets and investment decisions, politically taboo since Keynesianism was displaced as the official economic paradigm by supply side economics in the early Reagan years, has also crept back into view. Although official policy still confines government's role largely to manipulating interest and tax rates and raising levels of government debt to support corporate finance, should the U.S. economy continue to slump we can expect such voices to become louder.[16]

Besides its potential for shifting public opinion back toward recognition of the merits of macroeconomic regulation geared toward defending jobs and living standards, the range of economic challenges facing the U.S. also has the potential of weakening the influence of supply side economics among the intellectual and political elite as a whole. The right wing think tank infrastructure spent a generation wooing this political elite away from liberal economic and public policy approaches. It also poses a significant challenge to the neoliberal model that has dominated the Democratic Party's approach to economic management and its adoption of the right's rhetoric of downsizing government.[17]

The Crisis of Conservatism

The conservative movement has a lot on its plate. It is simultaneously facing a fiscal crisis of government, a crisis of ideology, a crisis of security credibility and a crisis of political appeal. It is also confronting irresolvable conflicts between the "military Keynesianism" model it used to refloat the economy in the 1980s and after 911, its tax-cutting ideology, and the electoral necessity of keeping its interest groups happy.

The economics of keeping the right's base constituencies—the anti-tax elite, suburban McMansion mortgagees and "Wal-Mart Republicans"— together is getting brutal.[18] Conservative politicians are being squeezed between the fiscal crisis produced by the massive 2003 Federal tax cuts, the billions required to support their corporate constituents (military and domestic) and the requirements of getting elected (e.g., funding the Medicare Plan B program and the 2005 highway bill).

Nevertheless, the right has not by any means been defeated in its crusade against government, and underestimating its willingness to push for even deeper cuts in public services and programs would be a mistake. Its propaganda has had an enduring effect on how people think about government.

Fifty-eight percent of Americans now want less government, according to progressive economist Jeff Faux.[19] Absorbing the lessons of Vietnam, Watergate, years of government corruption scandals, and fed for a generation on the bipartisan cant of "government is the problem, not the solution" and "the era of big government is over," people are skeptical about the role of government. They've absorbed the message, but see before their eyes problems they understand can only be addressed by a well run and adequately funded government. Polling suggests that although the right has successfully exploited and magnified the failures of government to shape public opinion against government, attitudes are still malleable and nuanced, and contain both positive and negative assessment of government.[20]

Nevertheless, four decades of intense effort by the right to vilify government has left a deep impression on the public, especially with regard to taxes, macroeconomic policy, wasteful spending, poor fiscal planning and how to address poverty and government burdens on the "little guy." Although some major social programs attract support when they are under attack, the public sector as a whole still has few defenders, especially when the carrots of lower taxation and more efficient services are held out as bait.[21] Reform has effectively been identified with downsizing and outsourcing.

Public debate remains dangerously trapped in a vocabulary and policy philosophy unsuited to dealing with the pressing economic and social problems facing the U.S. But as yet there is little broad public discussion on what the proper role of government should be, nor a clear economic paradigm on the progressive side to take the place of the bankrupt shibboleths of libertarian economics or the Bush administration's unfunded military- and pork barrel Keynesianism.[22]

The Privatization Frenzy

Although the centerpiece of the conservative strategy to kill off the New Deal—social security privatization—was turned back in 2005, a range of conservative think tanks and business interests are redoubling their efforts to push comprehensive deregulation and privatization at all levels of government, often disguised by the language of "outsourcing" (the new word for privatization), performance and efficiency.[23]

Privatizing public sector pensions and financial assets, public goods and public space (e.g., highways, education, water resources and public real estate) is at the top of the right's agenda, along with hard-wiring public revenues into corporate bottom lines through tax breaks, wasteful subsidies and the short-term cashing out of long-term public assets, such as highway tolls, for private interests.[24]

Some of the most important of these battles are taking place at the state and local level. The latest annual *Privatization Report* of the right wing Reason Foundation, *Transforming Government through Privatization*, proposes constitutional spending limits on state and local government, a radical expansion of outsourcing government services, and a massive sell off of public goods and assets. It also includes a call by Grover Norquist for a renewed drive to privatize social security, Medicare and public education and cut the size of government in half.[25]

The litany of government failures produced by the right's own governing record, and the deficits produced by its revenue and spending practices, are being used as a strategic weapon to set up further cutbacks in social services, fair wages and conditions for government workers, and to force the entry of private capital into hitherto inviolate domains of public services and the public commons. Understanding the strategy that the right has pursued to redefine the role of government is a critical part of developing a response, as is a forceful and clear restatement of the comprehensive case for effective government.

II. The Assault on Government from Progressivism to the Reagan Backlash

"The only way to have an honest government is to keep it poor."
—Georgia Gov. Eugene Talmadge, 1935

Discussion of shifting approaches to the role of government often begins with the New Deal and run through the Reagan era. But highly organized counterattacks against efforts to make government a dynamic and effective instrument for responding to public needs have been a constant theme in American history. And in each of these engagements, which were fundamentally affected by changes in the political economy of the U.S., the strategic battle to control the message in public debate, shape beliefs and dominate the war of ideas has played a central role.

An intense campaign was mounted from 1787 to 1789 by the Anti-Federalists, the coalition of landowners and small farmers who used limited government arguments to try and preserve a weak and underfunded Confederation government.

The enemies of Reconstruction after the Civil War produced newspaper screeds, learned essays and blockbuster books pitched at both the working class and the middle class intelligentsia that wove together themes—race, government extravagance, property rights and taxpayer abuse—used by small government conservatives ever since, including George Wallace and Charles Murray in more recent times. One of these books, *The Prostrate State* (1874) by onetime reformer James S. Pike, was used to cement an alliance between reformist Republicans and unreformed Confederates against newly created Southern governments and Federal social programs such as the Freedmen's Bureau.[26]

In one of the earlier known cases of what might be called neoconservative conversion, Pike's polemic attracted a nod of approval from the liberal editor of *The Nation* at the time, E.L. Godkin. Godkin was not alone among elite abolitionists in shifting to the right on the question of government's role in society. Arguments against the activist program of Reconstruction fed directly into Social Darwinist and anti-labor propaganda, as "free labor" ideology morphed into the "freedom of contract" arguments that business used for decades to resist government protection of the right to form unions and engage in collective bargaining. The 19th century liberal emphasis on antistatist individualism had a long future ahead of it.

As nascent unions began to agitate from the 1880s onward for an active role for government in curbing financial speculation, protecting the rights of workers to free association and enforcing an eight hour workday, they ran into concerted resistance not only from strikebreaking Pinkerton private guards financed by industry, but also by intellectuals in the universities and by the courts advancing these abstract notions of contract freedom and individual liberty.

The late 19th century Social Darwinists were the libertarians of their day, for whom the corporations were an advanced social form suited to a world governed by the "survival of the fittest." Yale professor William Graham Sumner, a frequent contributor to *The Nation* and the most influential American follower of Herbert Spencer, railed against a strong role for government in raising standards of living and taking on poverty and social problems.[27]

In the 1890s, Midwestern farmers teamed up with the growing labor movement in the Populist Party to push for more democratic government and sweeping government action to counter that decade's traumatic depression. The Populists, as journalist Bill Moyers recently reminded us, "invoked an American tradition as powerful as frontier individualism—the war on inequality and especially on the role that government played in promoting and preserving inequality by favoring the rich."

They were met with a well funded counteroffensive by the Eastern banks, grain elevator owners and middlemen led by Mark Hanna, a wealthy Ohio businessman with excellent Wall Street and media connections. Hanna, a hero of Karl Rove, masterminded William McKinley's successful campaigns against William Jennings Bryan, the Populist and Democrat standard-bearer.

Although the Populist movement was defeated politically, the politics of upheaval that threatened the destruction of capitalism elicited a more nuanced response. "Capitalism would have to be saved," Moyers tells us, "by reform and regulation," with government playing the major role. McKinley's vice president, Theodore Roosevelt, ran to the head of this Progressive parade when he assumed office on McKinley's assassination, attempting to develop a mediating role for government between capital and labor and waging a series of high profile battles against some of the railroad trusts.

Public attitudes toward the role of government became an ideological and political battleground. Sen. Robert La Follette, Sr., author of legislation permitting public employees to join unions (the 1912 Lloyd-La Follette Act), had pioneered the practice of making direct appeals to the electorate on policy issues in his previous post as governor of Wisconsin.

The National Civic Federation, a business-labor-professional coalition which Mark Hanna helped form, was created to publicize reform ideas as a counter to more radical ideas for addressing labor disputes, the power of economic oligarchy and social dislocation in the cities. The 1912 Taft Commission advocated performance budgeting.

The Role of Government and the Rise of the Policy Elite

The ground for the Progressive era (ca. 1900-1917) had been prepared not only by the Populists of the 90's, but also by the rise of the social sciences in America's leading universities and the formation of academic associations, which continued to play an important part in debates on the role of government.

These associations weighed in to press for an active role for government by engaging the politicians, judges and laissez faire publicists of the robber barons and their industrial descendants. Indeed the American Economic Association, which elected laissez faire economist Milton Friedman president in 1967, was founded in opposition to the iron grip of his philosophy, and stated in its 1885 draft prospectus that "we regard the state as an educational and ethical agency whose positive aid was an indispensable condition of human progress."

A new crop of research institutes arose to translate Progressive philosophy into practice through a focused effort of empirical research and policy engineering—generating specific proposals envisioning a powerful role for government in regulation and social welfare. The nexus of money, politics and policy did not begin with Rove:[28]

> *"The first generation of policy research institutions was founded around 1910, an outgrowth of the Progressive Era reform and the 'scientific management' movement. Established and sustained by private philanthropy, they operated in an era when government had few intellectual resources at its command, and they were a welcome adjunct to the then much-smaller public sector, often prodding government to assume new social responsibilities."*

This model was to heavily influence debate on the role of government for the next five decades, until the right wing think tanks formed in the 1970s began to supplant the role of mainstream and university-based social science and empirical research in policy making.

The Defeat of Progressivism and Assault on the New Deal

The Progressive era, which produced the Federal income tax, municipal and state reform movements, a legal reform movement to free government's hands to deal with corporate abuse and critical social problems (led by Louis Brandeis), the Federal Reserve System and food safety legislation, came to an end through a combination of resurgent business activism (e.g., the rise of organizations such as the National Association of Manufacturers), state repression (the Palmer Raids) and the widespread resurrection of the Ku Klux Klan in the 1920s not just in the South but across the country.

Debate on the role of government resurfaced with a vengeance when the conservative Harding, Coolidge and Hoover administrations, representing Eastern business interests, were elected in the 1920s. As a result of the financial and military demands of World War I, the Wilson administration had launched a major effort to separate politics and administration in the functioning of government, substantially raised income tax on the wealthy, introduced the first inheritance tax and imposed an excess profits tax on corporations.

Harding's treasury secretary, Andrew Mellon, attempted to uproot as much of the Progressive legacy as possible. His efforts to eliminate the inheritance tax were initially beaten back by the farm bloc, led by Senator La Follette, but the political ground had shifted. In a three way race in the presidential election of 1924, Calvin Coolidge ran on a platform of massive income tax cuts that conservatives consider a model of Reagan's "supply side" tax cut initiatives in the 1980s, and defeated both the Democratic nominee (John Davis, a corporate lawyer with close links to the Morgan interests) and La Follette.

La Follette had run on a program of government ownership of the railroads and the power industry, public management of natural resources, support for workers' right to unionize and bargain collectively, dissolution of monopolies and curbing the abuse of injunctions to attack labor. After his death in 1925, Mellon was able to push through a major reduction in the income tax, eliminate the Federal gift tax on the wealthy, and sharply increase the depletion allowance for oil and mining interests.

In the three years after the stock market crash of 1929, massive social dislocation swept through the country and underfunded state and municipal governments, some of which stopped paying their employees, were completely unable to cope. As social tensions rose and masses of the unemployed and displaced joined in demonstrations and mass actions across the country, even conservative voices began to warn of revolution.

Yet instead of pursuing a reflationary strategy, right wing organizations such as the National Economy League continued to agitate for even greater cuts in the Federal budget, especially on veterans' benefits, organizing chapters in 45 states and claiming a membership of 60,000. Roosevelt himself, who favored budget cuts, signed the National Economy Act in 1933 slashing the salaries of government workers and reducing veterans' pensions by 40%. The Veterans Bonus Bill that distributed $1.5 billion in cash to veterans in 1936 was passed over Roosevelt's veto. He was pushed forward by events to embrace deficit spending to finance a government response to the Depression.

During the 1930s, efforts by the Roosevelt administration to use the tools of government to cope with the effects of the Great Depression and save capitalism from a system-threatening upheaval from below were met by massive and sophisticated opposition from the business and legal community, both Democratic and Republican. Legal, political and policy obstacles were thrown in the way of Roosevelt's program for "positive government" by the right wing think tanks and activist organizations of the day.

The Edison Electric Institute and the National Lawyers' Committee of the American Liberty League waged a national propaganda campaign to paint Roosevelt's legislative initiatives as unconstitutional, publishing and disseminating a blizzard "private decisions" by eminent legal authorities declaring all aspects of the New Deal unconstitutional or illegal.

Rejecting the arguments of Louis Brandeis and Felix Frankfurter that fair labor practices and deficit spending were constitutional and necessary, Adolph Berle, the dean of modern corporation theory and an initial supporter of the New Deal, defiantly declared the "corporate revolution" permanent and weighed in against Roosevelt. After an initial period of cooperation, the newly founded Brookings Institution waged war on Roosevelt's policy initiatives.

In the 1936 presidential campaign, which was a referendum on FDR's policies, although Republican Alf Landon made the crusade against Social Security a centerpiece of his platform, the American Liberty League spent twice as much money agitating against it as did the Republican Party. The U.S. Chamber of Commerce, which through its Institute for Legal Reform has taken the lead in pushing "tort reform" and social security privatization today, bitterly opposed Roosevelt's social security bill. Playing the race card and backed up by the Hearst media machine, the anti-New Dealers, such as industrialist Pierre S. DuPont, also recruited Georgia Governor Eugene Talmadge, an arch-white supremacist and demagogue, to their cause.

Through the National Association of Manufacturers (NAM) and other organizations, the right pursued a complex strategy to influence people's beliefs on the role of government in settling labor disputes. NAM, recognizing the strategic role of the press and the new medium of radio, waged an aggressive campaign against the National Labor Relations Act and launched an extensive program to use the new science of public relations as a strikebreaking weapon.[29]

After World War II, NAM, under new and vigorous leadership, seized on the general public distaste for wartime regulations, divisions in the labor movement and a more conservative Congress to wage a renewed campaign to limit public support for government regulation and tear down or amend New Deal legislation. The right had changed its strategy from one of issuing pious homilies about individual responsibility and freedom to an all-out effort to target and shift public beliefs about government.

Flanking the Committee on Economic Development (a mainstream business coalition which accepted the need for Keynesian demand management to cope with Depression-level unemployment, and supported the minimum wage, Social Security and collective bargaining), NAM moved to change the public's attitudes toward government by reframing its message, commissioning polling and improving its message delivery apparatus.

"New hires," historian Andrew Workman tells us, "held advanced degrees in economics, law, and other fields or had extensive experience in public relations and advertising."[30] They faced a serious challenge, not only in countering the sophisticated lobbying efforts of the first generation of policy intellectuals who promoted social legislation and economic planning (originating with Roosevelt's "brains trust" and thereafter spreading through the Federal agencies), but from public belief in the necessity of active government. They had an uphill battle. According to Workman:

> "Most of the public believed that government intervention had saved the country from the Great Depression while businessmen had stood idly by spouting the old nostrums. What moved the public, poll data showed, was the prospect of economic security and heightened consumption, not the abstract notions of freedom that many NAM members then wished to sell."

The Right's Fifty Year Project and the Role of Government

By 1945 widespread acceptance of the need for government action to deal with the Depression, play a brokering role to stabilize labor relations, and mobilize to win the war had completely marginalized advocates of limited government. It had become common sense, not only among the policy elite but among the general population. One

British conservative complained that there was such general enthusiasm among economists for Keynes' *General Theory* "that those who do not accept its doctrines are to be regarded as intellectually inferior beings."

This consensus among the policy intelligentsia, many of whom were involved in administering the expanded regulatory state and for whom Keynesian economics was the new gospel,[31] set the stage for three decades of virtually uninterrupted expansion of government initiatives at all levels, funded by a booming American economy.

The list of these government initiatives is familiar, including the GI Bill (Roosevelt); a massive program of highway construction, the explosive growth of the military industrial complex and raising of the marginal top tax rate to 91% (Eisenhower); the launching of a major Federal public effort on affordable housing and aggressive extension of the Fair Labor standards act into the retail sector (Kennedy); the War on Poverty and Great Society programs[32] (Johnson); and creation of the EPA, OSHA and the indexing of Social Security to inflation (Nixon).

The Conservative Counterintelligentsia

The collapse of classical economics brought on by the Depression and the triumph of Keynesianism did not extinguish either the intellectual tradition of limited government or, needless to say, its support within important sections of the business establishment. Eventually a movement built around an aggressive assault on the New Deal view of the role of government would emerge, gain significant support in both academia and the corporate world, link up with new generations of activists and develop into a dominant movement that would turn social welfare and Roosevelt's slogan of "positive government" into dirty words.

The core pillars of this assault on government included:

- The re-branding of individualism to make it seem heroic rather than selfish and immoral
- An opposition to taxes
- A sustained drive to publicize government waste, bureaucracy and inefficiency, and

- Promoting the private sector and the "free market" as inherently better and more efficient than government.

The most important factor in this resurgence over the next five decades was the alliance between key figures in the corporate and financial establishment and what came to be called the conservative counterintelligentsia. These conservative and libertarian intellectuals were able to gain access to funding, space to do their intellectual work, media exposure, influence in the major parties (not just the Republican Party—Milton Friedman's monetarist policies were first applied by Jimmy Carter's appointee to head the Federal Reserve, Paul Volcker) and eventually become a presence in the corridors of power and administration.

In 1947, the Austrian economist Friedrich Hayek and a number of British and American economists from the anti-Keynesian factions at the London School of Economics and the University of Chicago formed the Mont Pelerin Society. This organization was in a sense the seedbed from which the broad philosophy of limited government that one sees everywhere today was reconstituted in modern form.

Hayek, an arch opponent of Keynes since the early 1930s, had created an intellectual commotion with his publication of *The Road to Serfdom* in Britain in 1944. The book was an ideological broadside against social democracy, which Hayek argued led in a direct line to tyranny.

The book painted all forms of government interference with market mechanisms as socialist and tyrannical, and maintained that there was no middle ground between totalitarianism and *laissez faire*. It was an instant hit with the right in the U.S. when it was published by *Reader's Digest* in April 1945, and General Motors even produced a cartoon version of the book in the early 1950s as part of its "Thought Starter" education series for its employees.[33]

The Mont Pelerin Society (MPS) was conceived of as an open ended seminar to create space for developing the intellectual tools to fight the rise of the modern administrative state and especially any form of government planning. It was also a vitally important forum for sharply debating ideological issues within the right, and for blending individualist philosophy, the art of economic statecraft and neoclassical economics.

The programs for postwar recovery and transition in the U.S. and Britain, and the Keynesian view that government could use the tools of budgetary adjustment, demand management and monetary policy to smooth out the capitalist business cycle, maintain full employment and promote growth and productivity was anathema to this group.

The history of the Mont Pelerin Society is too complex to recount here, but it played a significant role in creating a coherent set of intellectual beliefs, a venue for intellectual cross fertilization around which the ideological core of conservatism gelled; and in nurturing the relationships that underpinned the critical alliance between the British and American opponents of Keynesianism that would eventually lead to the Reagan-Thatcher partnership.

MPS, headquartered in Alexandria, Virginia, is still going strong and conducts annual high quality, low profile colloquia on economics and the issues of the day. Its treasurer is the Heritage Foundation's president, Edwin Feulner. Charles Baird, a member of the steering committee of the anti-labor Astroturf group Working Families for Wal-Mart, is a vice president and serves on its board of directors.

From Seminar Rooms to Living Rooms

Throughout the 1950s and early 1960s Milton Friedman, a co-founder of Mont Pelerin with Hayek, carefully laid the intellectual groundwork for an attack not only on government's role in regulating the economy (especially regarding consumption and the money supply), but on the very idea that government could be efficient and that its shortcomings could be remedied by timely and effective reform.

Talk of government reform was hardly in short supply in the mid-1960s. In fact LBJ had launched a major effort to tighten up Federal budgeting and programming practices,[34] was a strong promoter of what he called "creative federalism" and "management by objectives," privatized Fannie Mae in 1967 and took some tentative steps toward deregulating the trucking industry,[35] which the Carter administration was later to pursue with vigor and determination. But this challenge from the right was something new.

Despite the popular success of his writings, Hayek never produced a systematic critique of Keynes' *General Theory*. But others in the Mont

Pelerin group and especially in the wider Law and Economics movement centered on the University of Chicago, developed a full intellectual apparatus beginning from the 1950s onwards for documenting in every conceivable detail imagined and real government inefficiencies and distortion of markets.

They attempted to redefine capitalism's problems as an outcome of government interference with the free operation of markets rather than a failure of markets themselves. This "public choice" model came to dominate not only the social sciences, but also made extensive inroads in legal analysis and interpretation.

As George Nash, the foremost conservative intellectual historian of the right has pointed out, Friedman and his colleagues advanced the conservative cause by light years because they furnished "specific, arguable alternatives" for the first time to its movement publicists and politicians alike. This was policy engineering not for the purpose of reform or tinkering or efficiency—but for paradigm shift.

Friedman and the *National Review*-Mont Pelerin circle also furnished the conservative movement with media savvy and high octane business contacts. The right would never have gained any ground politically without undermining the broad popular belief in "positive government" that had been produced by government programs that people liked and were willing to pay for—the New Deal, the successful war effort, Federal Highway program, expansion of public education and so forth.

Friedman developed the bridging contacts with the business, media and political worlds that enabled conservative economics to break out of its academic ghetto at the University of Chicago and a few isolated economics departments and a scattered collection of movement journals.

In 1962, Milton Friedman published *Capitalism and Freedom*, a broadside against a strong role for government in economic management that accused government itself of being a significant contributor to market failure. The argument was a strategically sophisticated one, since the evident consequences of market failure underpinned both common sense and expert views of what went wrong in the Depression (then in living memory), and especially of Herbert Hoover's inadequate use of the tools of government to respond to the effects of the 1929 crash.

Throughout the 1960s Friedman became a familiar face on American TV through regular appearances on, e.g., William F. Buckley's PBS show "Firing Line," and later on during his high profile 1980 PBS series "Free to Choose," which ran during the election year in which "big government" was a central campaign theme of Ronald Reagan.

Reagan had also spread the corporate message of opposition to big government through his regular TV commentaries as a spokesman for GE in the 1950s and 1960s, and through his visible support for the Goldwater campaign, a focus for the resurgent conservative movement in 1964 that revived many of the themes of the Liberty League (Milton Friedman was an influential adviser to the campaign, which had a proto-think tank contingent led by William Baroody, Sr. of the American Enterprise Institute).

Reagan and Hayek were also regular guests on Buckley's PBS show, which provided a steady diet of programming on the hottest issues in a growing national debate on the proper role of government—such welfare, local control of education, and taxation.[36] If, as the columnist Robert Steinback has written, "the right has brainwashed an entire generation of Americans against believing that such a thing as good government is even possible," this effort began in the late 1960s and early 1970s.[37] In July 1967, Ronald Reagan appeared on Buckley's show to discuss whether big government was even making it impossible "to be a good Governor."

<u>Scapegoating Government</u>

The escalating costs of government programs to address poverty, unemployment and dislocation in the cities in the 1950s and 1960s did not result from some compulsion by New Deal social tinkerers to mindlessly generate new bureaucracies to distribute welfare, as the neoconservatives claimed. They were a byproduct of the massive postwar migration of the Southern and rural poor to the cities.

In fact, as Frances Fox Piven and Richard Cloward pointed out in *Regulating the Poor*, their seminal 1971 analysis of public welfare, "the relief response to these displaced people was minimal," but "the flow of poor people to the cities did not slacken because public money was withheld. They continued to come, and many continued to be unemployed or underemployed. As a result, a large mass of impoverished people built up in the cities."[38]

Yet the right, using an old trope in American politics, resurrected the racially charged concepts of the undeserving poor (Reagan's campaign blast at "welfare queens") as a device with which to fan popular resentment and achieve their longstanding desire to uproot the New Deal. Government became the scapegoat for capitalism's ills, and public programs became the issue rather than how changes in the U.S. political economy were to be effectively and fairly managed.

Despite the fact that both the American right wing and the liberal policy intelligentsia shared a commitment to traditional individualism (unlike, for instance, the European social democrats backing the welfare states being created on that continent), these programs were still attacked for undermining self-reliance and initiative among the poor.

This dimension of Johnson's War on Poverty reforms, which were premised on the idea that the poor lacked the skills and education to succeed, was buried in an ideological storm. The right emphasized handouts when talking to the middle class, and dysfunctional bureaucracy when talking to the policy elite.

Not only was government scapegoated, but the poor and unemployed themselves were as well. The neoconservatives also resurrected a cultural critique of poverty and responsibility that had a very old pedigree on the American right, though unlike the libertarians they did not want to banish government completely from the scene.

While the right has frequently claimed since the 1970s that Lyndon Johnson's War on Poverty and Great Society programs had to be abandoned because of their record of failure, in fact they attacked them straight out of the box without waiting for any results.

One of the most important vehicles for bringing the different ideological strands of the right together was the founding journal of the neoconservative movement, *The Public Interest*, which was started in 1965 by Irving Kristol and Daniel Bell. Kristol, a frequent contributor to the *Wall Street Journal* and *Fortune,* bridged the worlds of academia, business and journalism, and played a critical role in the 1970s and 1980s putting together the right wing think tank infrastructure through his Institute for Educational Affairs.

Shifting the Mainstream Paradigm to the Right

Kristol's well edited journal became a vehicle for veteran conservative ideologues and an intellectual hatchery for young activists out to test their ideas by engaging in polemical battle with the partisans of active government. The journal's articles used empirical research from the social sciences to assail the Great Society reforms and a strong role for government in solving social problems. This was a significant innovation in the art of permanent policy warfare on both the political and the intellectual levels, and eventually was institutionalized in the think tanks infrastructure of the right.

On the political level, articles from *The Public Interest* were important in two respects. First, they were influential in "shaking the faith of the middle classes in the welfare state, racial equality and social reform generally," as the late sociologist Steve Vieux put it. Secondly, *Public Interest* articles were used as a form of high class ideological leafleting as they were spread by well-connected neoconservatives and their allies through the political establishment to shift its views.

Although the articles were carefully argued, these connections were the decisive factor. Peter Steinfels captures the point:[39]

> *When Nixon, upon taking office, recommended to his cabinet a* Public Interest *article in which Peter Drucker asserted that modern government had proved itself incapable of doing anything effectively except waging war and inflating the currency, it obviously was not the case that Nixon just happened to be perusing* The Public Interest *one day and came across this interesting tidbit."*

On the intellectual level the creation of journals such as *The Public Interest* was a delegitimizing exercise directed at the mainstream policy institutions that shaped the role of government. Since mainstream social science played an important role in marking out the kinds of social problems that could be addressed by government intervention or regulation, attacks on the universities and think tanks where it was found, such as the Brookings Institution and RAND Corporation, undermined their legitimacy and called into question their commitment to the public good.

Many of the experts in these institutions had played prominent roles in the task forces that put together the legislative programs of the Great Society and staffed its dozens of new agencies and programs. In his Ann Arbor speech launching the Great Society LBJ had proclaimed "I'm going to get the best minds in the country to work for me."

Kristol, employing a term developed by the Yugoslav anticommunist activist Milovan Djilas, dubbed the policy intelligentsia a "New Class" that was only interested in furthering its own interests in promoting government bureaucracy. This set in motion the long campaign by the right to brand active government as an elitist affair and silence or marginalize an articulate constituency pressing for action to deal with the crisis of poverty, educational collapse and an acute housing shortage in the cities.

This theme jibed with similar attacks being directed at government officials by other conservative academics and ideologues. In 1971, George Stigler, a founding member of the Mont Pelerin Society and University of Chicago alumnus, published a journal article, "The Theory of Economic Regulation," which became the basis for analyzing government regulation by tying it to the rent-seeking behavior of interest groups.

The same year William Niskanen, the current president of the antigovernment Cato Institute and founder of the National Tax Limitation Committee, published a widely read book on the role of government that combined the rather old theme that bureaucrats exist to maximize budgets with a new one—that bureaucracy was a mortal threat to democracy because it took decision-making out of the hands legislatures at all levels of government. Niskanen proposed that all appropriations be required to receive two-thirds legislative approval.

"Maximum Feasible Participation"

Another of the key selling points of the Great Society programs, their at least formal acknowledgment of the need for community involvement if they were to succeed (the legislation creating the Community Action

Program mandated "maximum feasible participation"), also came in for a savaging from the rising neoconservative movement. Many of the circle's leading figures were involved in the furious and racially charged battles over community control in the New York City schools in the 1960s, which played a catalytic role in accelerating the neoconservative split from social liberalism.

Those who split turned their fire on the social scientists and politicians who remained committed to improving the programs, and on activists who criticized them from the left as a classic means of exercising social control over the poor.[40] Despite their insider positions in many of these policy making networks, they cultivated the image of outsiders. Media coverage of the Great Society programs also came in for abuse, most notably in the book *The News Twisters*, an early attack on alleged liberal media bias by Edith Efron, a devotee of libertarian icon Ayn Rand.

These polemical assaults in the late 1960s and early 1970s also threatened the funding and image of the mainstream think tanks, and shifted the parameters of the debate over the proper role of government to the right within these institutions themselves and among their funders. This had damaging effects beyond the egos of the policy gurus at these institutions who had no independent political base and could not respond in kind.

Kristol and his neoconservative cohorts went the mainstream think tanks one better by hitting them at their strong point—by questioning whether they were the bearers of empirical and scientific truth; and at their weak point—by employing a literate but polemical vocabulary that they could not respond to either because of the centrist protocols of objectivity and neutrality to which they adhered or because of temperament and inclination.

This asymmetry is still with us: the many thousands of university-based social scientists who research social problems and propose public policy or planning solutions can rarely compete for visibility in the media with the think tank communications capacities of the right, and risk the loss of funding or tenured positions if they challenge them on ideological grounds.

The Privatization Movement Takes Off

The mid 1960s to mid-1970s was also a period when the personal relationships and intellectual foundations underlying what became the think tank privatization juggernaut were laid. For instance, the current and longtime head of the Heritage Foundation, Edwin Feulner, studied at the London School of Economics in the 1960s under Peter Bauer, one of the leading lights of the "free market" economic counter-revolution, and worked part time for Ralph Harris, director of the anchor think tank for "free market" economics in the U.K., the Institute for Economic Affairs (IEA).

IEA was founded by Sir Anthony Fisher, a British businessman who helped fund some of the most important think tanks that would lead the intellectual and policy assault on the role of government from the late 1970s onwards, including the Manhattan Institute, the Pacific Research Institute and the Atlas Economic Foundation (whose mission under Leonard Liggio, a vice president of the Mont Pelerin Society, is to spawn yet more think tanks around the world).

Also working at IEA were the intellectual gurus who would eventually put together the privatization movement in both the United States and UK, including Madsen Pirie and two brothers, Eamonn and Stuart Butler. While they are hardly household names, the role that Pirie and the Butlers (who worked for Feulner at the influential Republican Study Committee in 1973) played in promoting the global movement for privatization and government outsourcing cannot be overstated. Pirie even authored a "training manual for intellectual subversives."[41]

Eamonn Butler now heads the influential Adam Smith Institute in Britain (which he co-founded with Pirie in 1977), which played a central role in the Thatcher government's privatization crusade.[42] He is also on the board of directors of the Mont Pelerin Society. Stuart Butler has been the chief policy figure at the Heritage Foundation since 1979 on role of government questions (he is now their vice president for domestic and economic policy), and has edited several volumes of Heritage's *Mandate for Leadership* series which have laid out in detail the policy blueprints for downsizing government since the Reagan administration.

From the early 1970's onwards, a sustained campaign to implement privatization began to gain ground, having migrated from the world of government contracting to the universities and then increasingly in the right's new think tanks.[43] Emanuel Savas, again hardly a household name, went from being the manager of urban systems at IBM Corporation, to holding a number of posts in the New York City government in the 1960s, to becoming the most widely quoted pro-privatization academic between 1972 and 1986.[44]

Savas published his first article on privatization in 1971, served as assistant secretary for policy development in HUD in the Reagan administration (see below), and was a member of New York State Gov. George Pataki's privatization council from 1995-2000. He is currently one of the foremost experts on privatization in the country, and serves on the editorial board of right wing Reason Foundation's *Privatization Watch*, founded in 1976 and now a leading source of policy elite thinking on the subject.

Big Government and the "Crisis of Democracy"

The efforts of Irving Kristol and other New York neoconservative intellectuals to shift the views of the mainstream intelligentsia on the role of government to the right through polemics and persuasion soon merged into a wider attempt to use the right's economic and media power to shift white middle class support away from government social programs (besides social security, which remained the "third rail" of American politics) in a more systematic fashion.

By the mid-1970s a note of serious concern, even panic, had entered discussions on the right about the trajectory of government. This was not only about escalating costs and questions of waste, bureaucracy and inefficiency that dominated annual budget battles over particular agencies and programs. The right continued to hammer away at these themes to shift middle class opinion away from government.

Beyond this, prominent voices at the top of the conservative legal and business establishments began to warn that the model of empowerment being generated by the new social movements and by government social programs was potentially shifting the locus of power in the American social order downwards. It was also about how the philosophy of "maximum feasible participation" being expressed in the streets in protests over the Vietnam War and racial injustice was eating away at the dominance and authority of the elite.

Three strategically important documents stand out in this counteroffensive against an active role for government:

- A highly influential strategy memo prepared by Lewis F. Powell (the future Supreme Court Justice) for the U.S. Chamber of Commerce on the threat to corporate dominance in society and the need to politicize the business community;
- A report on the relation between the role of government and the crisis of authority by Samuel Huntington; and
- A series of articles focused on the dangers of big government, followed by an influential book on staging a strategic counterattack, *A Time for Change,* by William E. Simon.

Powell's August 1971 memo, titled "Attack on the American Free Enterprise System," warned the U.S. Chamber of Commerce that the "American economic system" was "under attack" by the advocates of "statism," many of whom had penetrated government "as 'staffers' and consultants at various levels." Alarmingly, Powell notes, the attack was not confined to "the extremists of the left," but was "broadly based and consistently pursued," with "the most disquieting voices coming from perfectly respectable elements of society: the college campus, the pulpit, the media, the intellectual and literary journals, the arts and sciences, and from politicians." The media, Powell complained, "accords unique publicity to these critics."

Invoking the writings of Milton Friedman and Arthur Shenfield (a colleague of Hayek and leader of the Mont Pelerin Society), Powell proclaimed that the values of Western Society were under threat. He also argued that the traditional practices of corporate public relations and lobbying weren't enough to stem the tide, and that a much broader and more aggressive strategy was need that would target the influence of progressive political movements (the student antiwar, consumer, civil rights, feminist, environmental and labor movements).

Powell essentially outlined what was to become, over the next several decades, the infrastructure linking business, the right wing of the Republican Party and a network of think tanks:

"Strength lies in organization, in careful long-range planning and implementation, in consistency of action over an indefinite period of years, in the scale of financing available only through joint effort, and in the political power available only through united action and national organizations."

Powell's memo signaled a new stage in the politicization of the business community, and particularly in developing its capacity to engage in message-aligned and more coordinated policy action on issues of government regulation and social programs at the Federal, state and local level.

At the Federal level, the Business Roundtable, an association of the CEOs of major corporations, was formed in 1972 to enable the officers of top corporations to intervene more effectively in policy issues. State-level Business Roundtables have proliferated across the U.S. As a result, as Frances Fox Piven points out, "the business agenda became mainstream and even bipartisan political wisdom."

A year later, the American Legislative Exchange Council was formed, which went on to become the major vehicle for the corporate policy agenda at the state and local level. These new corporate organizing initiatives dovetailed with efforts by the Nixon administration at intergovernmental reform, including his proposals to replace the system of Federal grants with a revenue sharing plan, budget cuts, and consolidation of seventy programs into block grants to the states for urban development, education, law enforcement and manpower training. But Nixon's proposals were still primarily aimed at decentralizing and rationalizing government rather than substantially rolling it back.

Samuel Huntington's intervention was similar to Powell's, but was cast at a global level. Writing for the Trilateral Commission, he raised the question of whether the expansion of government social programs, the widespread political mobilizations of the 1960s and 1970s, decreasing confidence and trust in government (particularly "white confidence"), and a breakdown in respect for authority was making the United States ungovernable as a democracy.

He warned that a massive outpouring of democratic participation by previously marginalized groups had produced system overload, an excessive "growth in the bureaucratic, regulating and implementing 'output' institutions of government," which overwhelmed the "input" institutions of government (the decaying political parties and weakened presidency) and "produced doubts about the economic solvency of government." [45]

The Trilateral report also raised the issue that preoccupied Kristol and the other neoconservatives, the role of the intellectuals. "The advanced industrial societies have spawned a stratum of value-oriented intellectuals," the report maintained, "who often devote themselves to the derogation of leadership, the challenging of authority, and the unmasking and delegitimation of established institutions." Standing alongside them were "increasing numbers of technocratic and policy-oriented intellectuals," who along with the "adversary intellectuals" posed a serious problem for democratic government "in terms of its ability to mobilize its citizens for the achievement of social and political goals, and to impose discipline and sacrifice upon its citizens in order to achieve those goals."[46]

Nevertheless, Huntington takes heart from what he sees as a steady decline in political participation by the mid-1970s, and especially in a rising level of public dissatisfaction with the role of government, creating a potential split between the beneficiaries of governmental activity and taxpayers. "In 1972, for instance," Huntington comments, "for the first time, as many liberals as conservatives agreed with the proposition that government is too big."

Huntington pointed to a major shift in public opinion away from support for defense spending to support for social welfare programs, which he called "the welfare shift" and tied to an exploding Federal deficit and inflation. "The fiscal crisis of capitalism," he declared, "is a product of democratic politics." Huntington's solution to what he called an "excess of democracy" was a downsizing of democracy, which he reminds his readers "is only one way of constituting authority," and "is not necessarily a universally applicable one."[47] What was needed was a strategy of demobilization tied to the creation of a right wing counterintelligentsia.

The late William E. Simon played a central role in shaping the strategy by which the right helped shift public opinion against government, both as an architect of its think tank infrastructure from his perch as head of the Olin Foundation and as a board member of the Heritage Foundation.

Simon, who had been Gerald Ford's Treasury Secretary during the New York City fiscal crisis of 1974-75, published a key article in *Reader's Digest* (which had serialized Hayek's *Road to Serfdom*) titled "Big Government and Our Economic Woes," followed by *A Time for Truth.* This 1978 book (written with the assistance of Edith Efron; see above) urged the right to follow a political strategy directed toward rolling back government by specifically targeting what he saw as its key constituents and advocates—government employees, the recipients of public assistance and the university-based liberal and progressive policy elite.

Writing of his experiences in government during the energy crisis and the New York City fiscal crisis, which was a decisive turning point in the broader debate on the role of government, Simon laid into government assistance for the poor ("poverty may result from honest misfortune, but it also may result from sloth, incompetence, and dishonesty"), savaged the New Deal ("FDR corrupted the philosophical concept of freedom") and public sector unions, which he said had "a lethal impact on the New York economy."[48]

Simon also raised the party political question. Denouncing President Jimmy Carter for having authoritarian tendencies, Simon declared:[49]

> "The only thing that can save the Republican Party, in fact, is a counterintelligentsia. Without such a reservoir of antiauthoritarian scholarship on which to draw, it is destined to remain the Stupid Party and die. A political party which declares itself philosophically committed to freedom but allows an economic dictatorship to emerge in the United States without stirring up the fiercest political donnybrook in American history has asked for the oblivion to which it is presently being consigned."

This more aggressive approach prepared the battlefield for a shift of approach from reforming and improving government performance under Nixon and Carter to radically downsizing it. Carter had emphasized improved management, greater transparency, reform of the regulatory system and new partnerships and submitted eleven reorganization plans to congress to make the Federal government more efficient. He also deregulated aspects of the trucking, airline, rail, finance, communications and oil industries, and was subsequently recognized, if grudgingly, for his role on this even by some on the right wing.[50]

But the right wanted to break this paradigm of reform and make government the enemy.

Shifting the Mainstream: "Specific, Arguable Alternatives"

At the heart of this "fierce political donnybrook" was the role of government in macroeconomic regulation, the keystone of the New Deal order. In the run-up to his successful campaign for the Republican nomination and Presidency in 1980, Ronald Reagan and his advisers began to draw into their economic team the key figures that developed supply side economics, such as Jude Wanniski, Arthur Laffer and David Stockman. Coming on the heels of two deep recessions, the collapse of the Bretton Woods system, the weakening of the manufacturing sector, and the onset of stagflation, the election turned into a referendum on who could offer the best way out of what seemed to be a deep national downward slide.

Working with Reagan's economic policy coordinator, Murray Weidenbaum, Simon's counterintelligentsia was taking shape. Martin Anderson of the Hoover Institution assembled 500 intellectuals to back Reagan in the campaign, help staff the new administration, and flesh out what Nash called "specific arguable alternatives" that gave Reagan a coherent economic message and developed linkages with other issues. The creation of this strategic focal point also helped align the role of government messages of the corporate policy networks (the Business Roundtable and Business Council), emerging think tank infrastructure and politicians of the Republican right.

The supply siders' ideas had been creating a buzz in conservative economic and policy circles for a several years. Wanniski published his first article synthesizing this approach in Kristol's *Public Interest* five years earlier, and his bestselling *The Way the World Works*, conceived of as a refutation of Keynes' *General Theory*, in 1977.[51] Friedman's Chicago School was also by now a mature ideological movement. They were producing, along with their right wing British think tank counterparts, an extensive body of theory and literature touting the efficiency of markets by conservative public choice theorists and the Law and Economics movement (which busied itself trying to put quantitative measures on the economic efficiency of government regulation and allocation of property rights).[52] The conservative ideological counterrevolution was well along the way to securing its political dominance in mainstream economics.

Reagan and his advisers endorsed specific supply-side policy proposals, such as the Kemp-Roth tax cut bill (calling for an across the board 30% tax reduction) as a centerpiece of his campaign. His decision after the election to support Paul Volcker's take-no-prisoners monetarist policy at the U.S. Federal Reserve, using a tight money policy to fight inflation at all costs no matter what the consequences for unemployment (which rose to the highest level since the Depression), fundamentally changed the view of the role of government that had dominated the American scene since the 1930s. In the first year after Reagan was elected new investment and depreciation write offs were introduced, and Congress approved $140 billion in cuts in Federal social programs, more than half from income maintenance for the poor.

Supply side economics provided an additional dimension to the technical fix of monetarism. Not only was it pitched, like monetarism, as a macroeconomic solution to stagflation, but also added an enormous regressive tax cut for the wealthy into the mix (from 1978 to 1981 the top capital gains tax rate was reduced from 36% to 20%; the top marginal income tax rate was lowered from 70% to 28%).

The perception of unfairness had to be handled with care, but the issue of taxation enabled the right to create a populist opening. In 1978 the tax revolt had broken out in California, spurring the passage of Proposition 13, which sharply limited the property taxes used to finance government services. This handed the right wing a wedge issue with which to build support among the suburban middle class for what was essentially a massive tax break for the wealthy. Huntington had pointed to the suburban middle class as a key liberal constituency that consistently backed the expansion of government programs to deal with poverty, unemployment, urban development and education.

Reagan, "the Great Communicator," understood that to run and govern on a platform of supply side economics (which he approached with caution) he needed to complement the fringe ideas of the purists (even George H.W. Bush called it "voodoo economics") with a populist vocabulary that had mass appeal. This was the only way to begin permanently shifting the public's prevailing core beliefs in New Deal principles and a "mend it don't end it" approach to government.

The policy changes were critical. But to actually swing mainstream opinion the Reagan team wove together three rhetorical strategies, or "myths" as Sidney Blumenthal describes them in his account of the rise of Reaganism, that shifted the framing of government radically, from the benevolent if somewhat wasteful image people largely held since the Depression (although this was beginning to fray, as Huntington pointed out), to one where government was the devil incarnate.

These three myths were: 1) An FDR-like frontal assault on the pessimism and malaise that characterized the Carter years, based on an aggressive optimism rooted in the idea of a divinely anointed America, and a community of faith built on "neighbor helping neighbor"; 2) What Blumenthal calls "the way of Von Hayek," which "equates competition with liberty and economic planning with tyranny, individualism with prosperity and government with stagnation"; and 3) a full-throated denunciation of the demonic power of government, reinforced by the constant juxtaposition of New Deal government with the Soviet Union.[53]

"Better the occasional faults of a government that lives in a spirit of charity," FDR had declared, "than the constant omission of a government frozen in the ice of its own indifference." Reagan, by contrast, declared that "the nine most terrifying words in the English language are, 'I'm from the government and I'm here to help,'" and "the government's view of the economy could be summed up in a few short phrases: If it moves, tax it. If it keeps moving, regulate it. And if it stops moving, subsidize it."

Reagan's rhetoric echoed themes that had been developed by the neoconservatives, the Chicago School, Huntington and Simon—the inexorable growth of government programs once they were started, their creation of an unsustainable and false sense of entitlement, rights and dependency, and the "immorality" of the progressive surtax on the income of the wealthy. "Outside of its legitimate function," Reagan wrote, "government does nothing as well or as economically as the private sector of the economy."

These basic themes have remained the consistent foundation of the right wing's assault on government for a generation. Its ideology (a fusion of traditional conservatism, libertarianism and evangelical revival and renewal) operates simultaneously at the theoretical, policy and popular levels.

To drive these idea deep into the fabric of American political culture, the architects of the conservative counterattack on government, especially Kristol and Simon, began to put together, scale up and integrate the infrastructure needed to drive this message into the media and policy establishment.[54]

These new or revamped organizations provided

- Philosophical backup (the Claremont and Manhattan Institutes)
- Organizations that could provide policy engineering support (Heritage, ALEC, Cato, Reason, AEI).
- A counterattack in the media and academic worlds (the Intercollegiate Study Institute, National Association of Scholars, Reed Irvine's Accuracy in Media and Accuracy in Academia, Brent Bozell's Media Research Center)
- A strategy for putting together a conservative legal network to roll back the legal order put in place since the New Deal (the Federalist Society and National Legal Center for the Public Interest)
- A series of publications to inform the movement and provide an echo chamber (e.g., the *Heritage Insider*, *American Spectator*, *Commentary*, *World* magazine, *New Criterion*, and *Reason*)
- A strategic capacity to roll back the legislative and media influence of the labor movement (the U.S. Chamber of Commerce's National Chamber Foundation, National Federation of Independent Business, and National Right to Work Committee)
- A national publicity megaphone on the issue of government waste and inefficiency (Citizens Against Government Waste)
- The capacity for waging continual permanent warfare against taxation (Americans for Tax Reform, the National Taxpayers Union).

The assault on government in the 1980s was built primarily around the twin themes of tax cuts and privatization (with a hard focus on welfare and social services to stigmatize government), though there were also traditional government reform initiatives, such as downsizing of the General Services Administration from 35,000 to 21,000 employees and the spreading like wildfire of "Total Quality Management" through the Federal government (the Japanese-inspired quality circle concept).[55] In 1985-86, with Democratic Congressional backing, general revenue sharing was killed off in committee, and urban grants were made subject to sharp cutbacks under the Gramm-Rudman anti-deficit process. Contracting out was also well established at the state and local level by then, though not at the level that was to become commonplace a decade later.

The Reagan administration was able to draw on extensive backup from the Heritage Foundation and the National Federation of Independent Business (NFIB) to assist its government downsizing agenda. NFIB, which had played a key coordinating role on economic and regulatory legislative issues in the 1970s, assisted the Heritage Foundation in putting together its first 1100-page *Mandate for Leadership*, prepared as a blueprint for radical right wing economic action in the manner of Roosevelt's "first 100 days." NFIB also played a central role in the Congressional tax cuts of 1981 and 1986, and in defeating the Clinton administration's healthcare proposals in 1993-94.

Denouncing pragmatism, which it called "the new watchword of liberalism in retreat," *Mandate for Leadership* called for "the most comprehensive and far reaching program of regulatory reform ever undertaken by any administration in the nation's history."[56] Several months after taking office, Reagan issued an executive order requiring that agencies submit cost-benefit estimates to his budget director, David Stockman, for vetting, and empowered Stockman to virtually veto agency initiatives.

This regime was further tightened up under the George H.W. Bush administration, which imposed a regulatory moratorium and created, under Dan Quayle, a Council on Competitiveness. Initially designed to co-opt the issue of establishing an industrial policy, which was well beyond the right's conception of the proper role of government but was obtaining elite and popular support, the council became "a White House back-channel for businesses that wanted to fight environmental or worker safety regulations."[57] It was run out of Quayle's office by Irving Kristol's son Bill.

Cheap Grace

Mandate for Leadership also called for the formation of a national commission to recommend a radical scaling back of Federal regulations, which led to the creation of the Grace Commission (the President's Private Sector Survey on Cost Control in Federal Government) in 1982.[58] The commission, led by J. Peter Grace, produced a 47 volume, 21,000 page report proposing $825 billion in cuts and cost savings. Grace then founded Citizens Against Government Waste (whose toll free number is 1-800-BE-ANGRY) in 1984.

Grace also waged virtual war against religious progressives, in particular against the Catholic Bishops Conference over its issuing of a pastoral letter on poverty and the economy. For several generations, the mainline religious denominations had looked with favor on an expanded role for government to deal with social issues.

The letter was sharply critical of the American economic system for tolerating poverty and was seen as a counterattack by the Bishops against Reaganomics. The Cato Institute has estimated that Reagan presided over a real cut in non-defense discretionary spending of 9.5%. Grace's vehicle for conducting this religious defense of Reagan's slashing of government social programs, the Catholic Lay Commission, was funded and received staff support from the Olin Foundation, and was coordinated by Simon, Olin's president.[59]

Simon, who like Grace was an ultraconservative Catholic, was joined in this effort by Michael Joyce. Joyce, a member of the executive committee of the Grace Commission, went on from Olin to the Bradley Foundation, from where he played a central role in the radical scaling up of the think tank infrastructure from 1985-2002, and in putting together the welfare reform and "charitable choice" movements that eventually led to Bill Clinton's "ending of welfare as we know it" and the George W. Bush administration's "faith based initiative." Irving Kristol called him "the Godfather of modern philanthropy."

Michael Novak, an ex-liberal who like many neoconservatives had drifted to the right in the mid-1970s and joined the American Enterprise Institute, was the major intellectual force behind this counterattack by the friends of the administration against the Catholic Bishops. Novak called Simon's *A Time for Truth* "the first libertarian book that really sang for me."

The Reagan administration also began to move aggressively against the public policy groups of the left, cutting off the funding and access to the Federal government that had enabled them to drive public debate in a progressive direction and that so frightened and infuriated Powell, Huntington and Simon.

For instance, in addition to proposing Enterprise Zones, targeting Community Development Block Grants for elimination, and aggressively promoting the involvement of the private sector in neighborhood development, the Department of Housing and Urban Development scaled back the role that local community and consumer groups played in its programs, and eliminated the Federal Neighborhood and Consumer Protection Office. "I think we had a little trouble here once these neighborhood organizations had access to Washington," HUD secretary Samuel Pierce commented.[60]

A parallel effort to undercut the political base for progressive politics by cutting back municipal budgets was emerging in the think tanks, primarily the Manhattan Institute and the Reason Foundation, which became hubs for developing the policy engineering (specific arguable alternatives) positions of the right on the cities. Major books were coming out thick and fast on changing the role of urban government. Reason's founder Robert Poole published a widely distributed sourcebook in 1980 on the subject, *Cutting Back City Hall*, which won him an appointment as an adviser on privatization to Reagan's Office of Policy Development.

The following year libertarian economist James T. Bennett published *Better Government at Half the Price* with Manuel Johnson (Bennett is now director of the John M. Olin Institute for Employment Practice and Policy and editor of the anti-union *Journal of Labor Research*).

The year after that, in 1982, Emanuel Savas (see above) published *Privatizing the Public Sector: How to Shrink Government* while serving as assistant director for policy studies under Pierce. Savas resigned from his post when the Justice Department found that he had used government staff to edit and proofread the updated manuscript, which he had originally prepared in 1978 for what became the Manhattan Institute.[61] The *New York Times* commented dryly that Savas "not only wrote the book on 'Privatizing the Public Sector,' but apparently practiced it." Undeterred, Savas published a landmark how-to book, *Privatization: The Key to Better Government* in 1987, and *Privatization and Public Private Partnerships* in 2000, which have become standard texts in university public administration courses.

Savas' Social Darwinist approach to the cities is summarized by Mike Davis as follows:[62]

> *"Savas argued that federal urban policy had been a complete failure and that cities had to be weaned, however brutally, from their artificial dependence upon Washington. (…) [Savas] advocated competitive acceptance of the new discipline of the world economy and a thoroughgoing privatization of local government services. (…) Thus the 1982 National Urban Policy Report drafted by Savas envisioned an inter-urban war of all against all as cities were advised to 'form partnerships with their private sectors and plan strategically to enhance their comparative advantages relative to other jurisdictions.'"*

Savas recently published a comprehensive study of privatization comparing the experiences of New York under the Giuliani administration with other cities such as Indianapolis and Phoenix, running through the full panoply of privatization devices including competitive sourcing, contracting, divestment, franchising, vouchers, leasing, and managed competition in park and fleet maintenance.[63]

The Political Turn: Cracking Open the Liberal Consensus

Toward the end of Reagan's second term the conservative movement was nearly in open revolt over what it saw as the administration's surrender on the central issue of redefining the role of government through downsizing and ending deficit spending. As a result of deep tax cuts, a recession and a major increase in military spending, the budget deficit had ballooned from $40 billion to $149 billion over the course of the two Reagan terms.

Stuart Butler of the Heritage Foundation charged that a newly appointed bipartisan National Economic Commission created in the run-up to the 1988 elections was a stealth device by the administration to prepare the ground for yet more tax increases to deal with the deficit, kicking the can down the road for a new administration (this fed into the famous "read my lips, no new taxes" pledge that George H.W. Bush made during the presidential campaign that year).

The problem, as Butler saw it, was not a lack of determination, but that the administration had been defeated because it had failed to change the "underlying political dynamics that favor increased Federal spending," specifically the influence of pro-spending constituencies with politicians:[64]

> "Conditions must be created in which demand for government spending is diverted into the private sector. This is the beauty of privatization. Instead of having to say 'no' to constituencies, politicians can adopt a more palatable approach to cutting spending. They can reduce outlays by fostering private alternatives that are more attractive to voters, thereby reducing the clamor for government spending. Changing the political dynamics of spending in this way is the secret of privatization."

The concept of privatization had gained important institutional support from the private sector and within government. The corporations had formed a Privatization Council in 1985,[65] and the American Legislative Exchange Council had a privatization working group that brought together key players to set priorities and draft legislation.

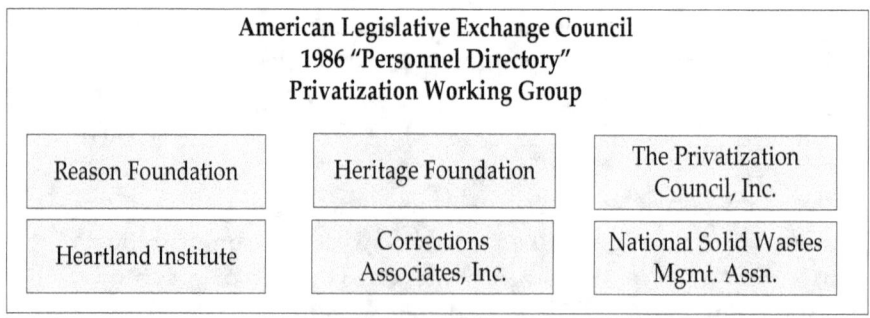

American Legislative Exchange Council 1986 "Personnel Directory" Privatization Working Group		
Reason Foundation	Heritage Foundation	The Privatization Council, Inc.
Heartland Institute	Corrections Associates, Inc.	National Solid Wastes Mgmt. Assn.

On the government side, Reagan had appointed a Presidential Commission on Privatization in 1987 that made seventy recommendations.

But from the perspective of the right wing think tanks the administration had few results to show for itself. It had pushed harder on budget cutting and deregulation than on privatization and as a result was treading water on the central issue of redefining the role of government.

The Heritage Foundation considered progress on this front so slow that it began a 1986 "Primer" on privatizing Federal services with the words "a new word—*privatization*—has entered the lexicon of federal budget making. Put simply, privatization means the transference of federal assets or activities to the private sector."[66] Robert Poole at the Reason foundation considered the "non-Thatcher-like remit of the commission" so weak that he formed a Shadow Privatization Commission that issued its own report.[67] Fred Smith of the Competitive Enterprise Institute charged that privatization "had quickly been captured by the forces of the status quo in and out of government."

In a somewhat bitter but astute article analyzing the reasons for failure, Fred Smith tore into the Reagan approach for failing to develop an effective strategy to take the offensive against core Democratic constituencies. Building on the writing of Heritage's Stuart Butler (especially his 1985 *Privatizing Federal Spending*) and Madsen Pirie (who had just published *Dismantling the State*, a handbook for his American audience),[68] Smith argued that in order for a privatization proposal to "make it through the political process" it is necessary to "create a viable privatization coalition" in favor of it. A frontal assault would not work.

"Thus a top priority," Smith wrote, "should be to identify Democratic senators and representatives who might be persuaded to support privatization and convince them to take the lead on the issue."[69] The liberal think tanks were also targeted, as by then the progressive community and mainstream planning establishment were beginning to respond in print to the privatization bandwagon.

These responses included Paul Starr's cogent and comprehensive "The Limits of Privatization," and the National Association of Public Administration's 1989 report *Privatization: The Challenge to Public Management.*[70] That year the Olin foundation provided funding to the Brookings Institution for a book on education vouchers, and throughout the 1990s to the program on education policy at Harvard's Kennedy School of Government because, in the words of Olin's executive director, James Piereson, "we were interested in getting these ideas ensconced at liberal places."[71]

Butler also picked up on Pirie's approach as a political strategy for detaching key elements of the coalition supporting Federal, state and local government programs, of "using privatization to reshape the interest group environment," as Jeffrey Henig puts it.[72] Pirie himself followed up this discussion with several books, widely discussed in the think tanks, on how to identify and target key constituencies that might support or oppose privatization, and how to break down privatization initiatives on tough issues, such as education vouchers, into manageable stages that could gradually neutralize opposition.[73]

This involved a piecemeal strategy of privatization by buying off, co-opting or defeating key constituencies in smaller government programs and then broadening out the "public choice" framework into core areas of the welfare state such as social security, healthcare and education, and core government services such as water provision and road construction and maintenance.

The objective, quite explicitly discussed, was to crack the core of liberal, New Deal unity on active government in order to isolate and defeat labor unions, its most powerful constituency. That the Reagan administration's deregulation efforts succeeded "indicates that even when strong worker opposition exists to a specific policy, it can prevail," Smith argued. The unions were "overcome by a strong political coalition of user groups (business and consumer)," supported by the research of think tanks "indicating the negative effects of regulation."[74]

He also proposed "buying out the interest groups" (the most important being the public sector unions) by allowing government employees to form their own companies to carry out government functions, and introducing user charges by tougher enforcement of existing OMB regulations to win users over to privatization:

> *"Since in most cases the costs of government-provided services exceed those of private providers, users of government services would find themselves facing greater costs than if the service were provided privately. Thus, users would become a prominent*

lobbying force for privatization — as in fact they did for transport deregulation."

Smith argued that the administration had used the issue effectively in its electoral battles, but lost the war by not following through with a political strategy to neutralize or split the opposition to privatization once it was in government. He also accused the administration of not "crafting viable privatization policies," but instead ignoring those that had come out of the think tanks (such as the Heritage Foundation's proposal, in its 1984 *Mandate for Leadership II*, to privatize military commissaries) and of "sending the idea haphazardly into the political process."

Smith also criticized the administration for falling down on framing, which it is interesting to note the right was talking about in its strategy documents nearly two decades before this seized the imagination of progressives and liberal Democrats after the 2004 elections:

> *"Perhaps one of the most important advantages of presenting a comprehensive policy plan is the ability to 'frame the issue' for each privatization attempt. For example, privatizing air traffic control should be presented as an attempt to 'improve air safety.' Selling the Tennessee Valley Authority (TVA) should be presented as an issue of 'increasing local accountability and improving the service.'"*

For Smith, framing without the networking, policy infrastructure and a willingness to take risks on issues that would damage the opposition was a losing strategy. A successful strategy would require the right to mobilize its base on the issue through organizing, and develop its own counter-constituencies favoring privatization with the help of the right wing infrastructure.

To defeat the New Deal coalition, Smith argued, the right needed to systematically develop a counter coalition of organizations and interests that had an economic stake in privatization and innovative strategies. The turn to outsourcing and performance reviews as a political strategy — they had long been there as administrative tools, advocated by both the 1912 Taft and 1949 Hoover commission reports — was born.

III. From "Reinventing Government" to the Bush Administration

"The era of big government is over"
President Bill Clinton, 1996

By the time Bill Clinton took office in 1993, the right had effectively reframed the debate on the role of government across a range of issues through a series of negative campaigns, sustained by its growing infrastructure, on taxation, the war on poverty, public education, health care, retirement security, the environment, and the state of the cities.

The right's successful crusade against Clinton's proposal to create a national health insurance program in 1993-94, which was explicitly framed in big government versus "free market" terms, reinforced and amplified this message. It also spurred a higher level of coordination and tactical agility on the right on key issues defining government's role, such as taxation, environmental protection and corporate regulation.

Moreover, it helped knit together elements of the business-think tank-politician coalition that achieved power in the next decade and moved to defund or privatize major New Deal and Great Society programs such as Social Security and Medicare.

Grover Norquist's weekly Wednesday strategy meetings of conservative activists began as a gathering to fight Clinton's plan, which Norquist feared would reestablish public support for active government for decades. Indeed Hillary Rodham Clinton called it "the Social Security Act of this generation, the reform that would establish the identity of the Democratic Party and be the defining legislation for generations to come."[75]

In spite of the right's efforts, however, public opinion on the role of government remained ambivalent and more nuanced than its ideologues claimed. Polling conducted in the mid 1990s found that on the central issue concerning the role of government in the Reagan-Bush I years, deregulation, more than 60% of the public still strongly supported Federal workplace, health, food and drug safety regulations.[76] Support for social security and Medicare was at the same or higher levels.

Nevertheless, the right's campaigns against government had clearly had an impact. Pollsters found a striking loss of confidence in government over the previous two decades. The racially-charged campaigns against welfare waged by the New Right in the 1980s, which Clinton echoed by making "ending welfare as we know it" a campaign theme, had further driven down support for programs that were once widely popular.

The public also viewed government as more of an obstacle than a help in achieving the American dream, and maintained a strong preference for focusing programs at the state rather than the Federal level. There was also strong support for improving government management and performance.[77]

Reinventing Government

Shortly after taking office, President Clinton launched a major initiative to "reinvent" the Federal government to improve its performance. The concept, inspired by Tom Peters and Robert Waterman's highly popular book, *In Search of Excellence*, had been popularized by two writers, David Osborne and Ted Gaebler, in their 1992 bestseller *Reinventing Government: How the Entrepreneurial Spirit Is Transforming the Public Sector*, and later on by a follow-up book by Osborne and Peter Plastrik, *Banishing Bureaucracy*.

Osborne's entrepreneurial approach to reforming government, in which iconoclastic, rule breaking and innovative managers—"change agents"—play the hero's role in battling bureaucracy, became the template for both Clinton terms. Privatization was central to Osborne and Gaebler's reinvented government. "It makes sense to put the delivery of many public services in private hands" they wrote in their 1992 book.

Clinton assigned Vice President Gore to oversee the reform project under the auspices of an intergovernmental task force, the National Performance Review, which issued a major report in September 1993,

From Red Tape to Results: Creating a Government that Works Better and Costs Less and a follow-up in 1995, *Common Sense Government.*[78]

The Gore reports described four core activities to pursue: *downsizing* (reducing the size and number of agencies, their programs, and staff); *streamlining* (simplifying the procedures involved); *restructuring* (reforming agencies structurally to better serve their missions); and *privatizing* (spinning off functions to the private sector that are better accomplished there). They advocated four principles: "cutting red tape," "putting customers first," "empowering employees to get results," and "cutting back to basics."

President Clinton asked Gore, as part of the NPR, to identify additional programs that could be reinvented, terminated, privatized, or sold. The agency reviews identified a long list of potential functions to privatize including the Seafood Inspection Service, The OSHA and MSHA Accreditation Process, The Office of Personnel Management's background investigations service (that became USIS), the DOL Penalty and Debt Collection and the Federal Helium Program.

The commission's final recommendations called for "more competition, more privatization." The report embraced the idea of "government monopoly" first articulated by privatization ideologue E.S. Savas in the 1970s and called for "the introduction of competition to reduce the monopolistic control many governments have over their customers."

Civic Democracy vs. Entrepreneurialism

As noted above, there is a long history of efforts by politicians and public administrators to reform government, and many of the recommendations by the Gore Commission fell into this category. In this sense its claims to establishing a unique new paradigm for the role of government, and indeed those of Osborne and Gaebler, were overblown.[79]

What was different, however, was that a fundamental shift had occurred in the underlying conception of the proper role of government held by the liberal leadership, as represented by the Democratic Leadership Council and the centrist New Public Management

Movement. As Clinton later remarked, "reinventing government was a New Democratic idea."[80]

Samuel Huntington was not the only one concerned about the social movements of the 1960s and 1970s slipping the bounds of party control. The DLC, comprised essentially of neoconservatives who remained within the Democratic Party instead of leaving it, made a rejection of the politics of the feminist, civil rights and antiwar movements, and the traditional labor focus of the party, its central purpose.

The civic democracy approach, which Democrats and moderate Republicans had largely supported for decades, receded from view in the Gore Commission report. As Laurence Lynn describes it, this is a "town meeting" approach to governance that "fosters inclusiveness, deliberation, and responsiveness through the dispersal of authority, multidirectional accountability, an empowered public, and the primacy of the democratic process."[81]

Instead, Lynn writes, the entrepreneurial "competitive government" model of the Gore commission report evoked the "centralized and businesslike approach," of "an enterprise increasing its earnings and market share through successful product development, technological advances, and a productive and well deployed work force." The business managerial vision of the "reinventing government," he comments, stands in awe of business practice but this "is carefully concealed." Its proponents take "great pains" to say "that government isn't a business—but the spirit, as the Gore report acknowledges, is the Hamiltonian one of looking to successful executives."

This is reflected in Gore's choice of the word "customer" to describe the recipients of government services. "By 'customer' we do not mean 'citizen'," the report declares in its introduction. As Lynn remarks, "in Gore's conception, not only must government redefine citizens as customers, but citizens must redefine themselves as customers demanding a government 'worth what they pay for it.'"

Lynn rejects this notion:

> "Public policy implementation, is not, in fact or even
> metaphorically, a business; putting customers first is not the
> same as putting the needs of citizens first. Fairness, just

treatment, opportunity, security of person and property, participation in social deliberations, rule of law: these are the generic goals of government. They cannot be achieved solely through markets nor measured by highly compressed algorithms."

The approach that the administration followed thus fell firmly into channels laid down by the right in the late 1980s by emphasizing budgetary savings, efficiency, staffing cutbacks, performance reviews, and deregulating state and local governments. Indeed Edward Crane of the Cato Institute said that the Gore report essentially repeated the findings of Reagan's Grace Commission, which also emphasized efficiency and administrative control. Clinton justified the "reinventing government" initiative by pointing to the elimination of 300,000 Federal jobs, 250 programs and $137 billion in cost reductions.[82] His communications director, George Stephanopoulos, worried that allowing Gore to take this tack this would "unleash more deficit reduction mania," as Bob Woodward put it, but Clinton overruled him.[83]

Performance as Privatization Catalyst

On the question of privatization, however, the change from the Reagan-Bush administrations was clear—but in the direction of greater privatization. Writing in 1997, the Heritage Foundation's Ron Utt (who had been Reagan's "privatization czar") praised Clinton for pursuing "the boldest privatization agenda put forth by any American president to date," and noted that his proposals were "virtually all drawn from recommendations made in 1988 by President Reagan's Commission on Privatization."[84]

In the 2006 edition of the Reason Foundation's annual *Privatization Report*, Robert Poole declares that "the Clinton administration's privatization successes exceeded those of Reagan." Poole points to the selling off of the national petroleum reserve, billions of dollars worth of the electromagnetic spectrum, the competitive contracting of hundreds of airport control towers and military base functions.

However, unlike in Western Europe where privatization involved major industries that had been nationalized by social democratic governments before and immediately after World War II, in the United

States it has primarily involved a major shift toward private contracting and competitive bidding for government services.

In the "reinventing government" approach of the Clinton administration, Osborne's concept of "competitive government" was closely tied to the creation of "performance based organizations" throughout government, and the widespread requirement of performance reviews at all levels.

The "PBO" concept had originated in the "Next Steps" program in Britain, launched in 1988 by the Thatcher government as a process for deepening privatization initiatives beyond de-nationalizing major industries and into government services. Next Steps separated policy functions from service delivery functions, which were to be run along commercial lines.

In 1993, as part of the "reinventing government" initiative, the Government Performance and Results Act (GPRA) was signed by Clinton. The "Results Act," as it was called, mandated that agencies produce strategic plans, set goals and monitor implementation—in many cases producing a steady stream of targets for the pro-privatization networks to take aim at, amplify and 'solve' through their well-paid government consulting groups.

Clinton's commitment to reducing or at least containing the federal personnel head count—such as his backing of the 1998 FAIR Act requiring agencies to declare their activities inherently governmental or subject to privatization—opened up space for hiring private contractors.[85] This set the stage for Clinton's successor, George W. Bush, to fill the hiring slowdown with contract workers: during Bush's first term the number of federal contract employees dramatically increased, from an estimated size of 5.2 million in 2002 to more than 7.6 million in 2005.[86]

The "Results Act" originated in efforts by the late Republican Senator William Roth of Delaware (a co-author of the Kemp-Roth 25% income tax cut of 1981) to pass a similar bill in 1990.

After the Republican takeover of the House in 1994, the situation took an even sharper turn to the right. "What's caught this city, the political class and the media class by surprise is that the political conversation has totally changed its terms," Terry Eastland, a former Reagan Justice Department official said. "The entire conversation is, 'How do we limit and downsize government?'"

Majority leader Dick Armey and speaker Newt Gingrich pushed aggressively for GPRA's implementation. "The Results Act" has since spawned a conservative "government performance" industry of think tanks, lobbyists and corporations promoting competitive sourcing, public-private partnerships, performance reviews, public asset sales, etc., that has spread throughout government at all levels.[87]

The performance reviews mandated under GPRA were spun in the media by the Gore commission and its successor, the National Partnership for Reinventing Government, as a means of cutting down waste and empowering frontline managers and workers to innovate and improve government services.

In practice, however, the performance reviews became the focus of a political and economic battleground between the right, which wanted to push its privatization and contracting-out agenda even further, and the Clinton administration, which was attempting to triangulate between the privatizing and downsizing agenda of the right and its own political base.

This balancing act is well captured in a May 1996 report issued by the Secretary of Labor Robert Reich's "Task Force on Excellence in State and Local Government through Labor-Management Cooperation." Designed to restore public faith in government and replete with mixed polling data on how the public viewed privatization,[88] the document sought to identify common ground between advocates and opponents of government reform efforts.

"Privatization is not a panacea," the report declares, " and "the public's bottom line is not that government should do fewer things than it now does—but that it should get the job done with less waste, less bureaucracy and a keener sense of the people paying the bill." It also highlighted what it saw as successful efforts by conservative politicians such as Indianapolis Mayor Stephen Goldsmith to galvanize labor-management cooperation.

Above all, the Clinton administration pursued a politically "balanced" approach to government reform. On the one hand, Secretary Reich gave labor unions a seat at the table in National Partnership Councils to move labor-management cooperation forward. On the other hand, other parts of Clinton Administration were doing deep agency–by-agency analyses to identify privatization targets that drew praise from the Heritage Foundation and the Reason Foundation. And in the middle were genuine efforts to make government more efficient, consistent with previous government reform efforts.

Counterattack: "Revolution at the Roots"

The right responded to the Clinton initiative on several fronts. First, its policy think tanks, such as Heritage, Cato and Reason Foundation aggressively challenged the Clinton administration's implementation of the "Results Act," continually criticizing the quality of its performance reviews and competitiveness measures. This theme was picked up by George W. Bush in the 2000 election campaign.

The right's policy specialists also questioned the administration's figures, for example claims by Clinton and Gore to have cut back the number of government employees. "Reinvention," they said, had produced an insufficient "body count."[89] Anti-labor think tanks, such as the Public Service Research Council, an offshoot of the National Right to Work Committee, weighed in against the role of the public sector unions in the National Partnership Councils.

The central focus of the attack, however, was ideological, and was directed at discrediting the "excellence in government" model developed by Osborne and Gaebler that lay at the heart of the Clinton initiative and was gaining widespread support in the field of public administration and in state and local government. This was the battle for the allegiance of the mainstream intelligentsia that Powell and Simon had advocated. Unlike in the 1970s, however, by the mid-1990s the right had a fully developed infrastructure adept at spinning and disseminating its message to a mass audience through the media and politicians and to the policy elite.

The ideological counteroffensive was led by William D. Eggers and John O'Leary of the Los Angeles-based Reason Foundation, which with substantial funding from the Charles G. Koch, Olin, Sarah Scaife,

Bradley and other right wing foundations has grown into the right's main laboratory for generating privatization proposals and training the foot soldiers who staff the privatization and outsourcing industry.

Eggers co-authored two books that were intended the stop the "reinvention" wave in its tracks, *Revolution at the Roots* (with O'Leary) in 1995 and *Governing by Network* (with Stephen Goldsmith) published by Brookings in 2004. In 1995 William Simon's Olin foundation contributed $20,000 for the marketing and promotion of *Revolution at the Roots*, and the JM Foundation produced another $15,000 to promote the book through the network of state think tanks being put together by right wing funder Thomas A. Roe under the aegis of the State Policy Network.[90] Eggers won both the State Policy Network's Roe Award and the Atlas Economic Research Foundation's Sir Anthony Fisher Award the following year.

A former policy analyst with Heritage who headed the Reason Foundation's Privatization Center, Eggers accused the Clinton administration and its intellectual allies in the "Reinventing Government" and New Public Management Movement of tinkering with administrative reforms, managerial initiative and decentralization. These approaches focused, according to Eggers and O'Leary, not on what government does but only on how it does it. They did not push sufficiently to cut back government to its core functions.

By this they meant not only government's pre-New Deal functions but its 18th century functions. They endorse Adam Smith's minimalist view of the role of government as protecting the public, preventing injustice, and building and maintaining public works that the market would not or could not provide.

While talking about efficiency and rhetorically distancing themselves from the "cynics" who think nothing can be done to improve government, in *Revolution at the Roots* Eggers and O'Leary depict government as a completely negative force. Only outside pressure from an outraged public or from crusading chief executives bent on shrinking government (not just on reinventing it or making it excellent) offers the possibility of change.

The coalition that Eggers and O'Leary suggest would be necessary to secure such an agenda accorded perfectly with the right's overarching political strategy of fusing Grover Norquist's tax revolt/tax cap movement, Newt Gingrich's new devolution and downsizing majority in Congress, and the new cohort of conservative politicians then taking power in the statehouses and municipal offices. *Revolution from the Roots* was the Contract for America and Compassionate Conservatism expressed in the vocabulary of public administration.

More recently, it has added the capacity, though Americans for Limited Government (ALG), to "Swift Boat" public employees by running crude attack ads across the country demonizing public sector workers. ALG is headed by Howard S. Rich, a New York City real estate investor who is driving the extreme anti-government agenda of the corporate-backed Club for Growth down into the states and cities as head of its Club for Growth State Action program. Ed Crane, head of the Koch-funded Cato Institute, is on ALG's board of directors, and Rich is on Cato's board.

While calling for the "radical devolution" of Federal programs to the state level, Eggers and O'Leary call for severely limiting the role of state and local government in shaping economic development, restricting its role to cutting taxes and regulation, and opposing subsidies and inducements to attract investment.

Their favorite "change agents" were the new heroes of the Republican economic right. Stephen Goldsmith of Indianapolis, Rudolph Giuliani of New York, Brent Schundler of Jersey City and New Democrat mayor John Norquist of Milwaukee in the cities; and John Engler of Michigan (now head of NAM), Tommy Thompson of Wisconsin and George Allen of Virginia in the statehouses.

At the Federal level they advance the view, more frequently heard in the precincts of the far right populist movement than in the field of public administration, that under the Tenth amendment—which provides that all powers not assigned to the federal government are reserved to the states or the people—"most Federal activities dealing with domestic issues such as education, poverty relief, cultivation of the arts and sciences, business loans, and so on, are unconstitutional."[91]

The response came swiftly. In a debate with Eggers and O'Leary at the Pacific Research Institute, *Reinventing Government* co-author Ted

Gaebler shot back by reminding them that active government had been created to correct "rampant unfettered abuses of capitalism."

What the right was trying to do, Gaebler said, was not to reinvent government, but to reinvent politics by promoting term limits and constitutional amendments that ruled out democratically mandated forms of government action the right didn't like. As for cutting back to core functions, he remarked that there was no workable definition of core functions, which differed radically from government to government across the world and couldn't be prescribed according to some ideological template.

He also rejected as undemocratic the view that government should be run on corporate lines.

> "Nobody in a democracy wants governments to be run like a corporation, with policy decisions being made overnight, behind closed doors, by one person, strictly for the basis of profit. In our democracies, we want decisions to be made far more openly over a longer period of time, in a far more messy way, with profit maybe being one of the motives but not the only one."

Gaebler also refuted Eggers' and O'Leary's notion that change could only come from the outside by public pressure and crusading downsizers, saying that experience at every level of government, and with many kinds of outsider models had shown repeatedly that "the only way that really works is to empower public employees at all levels," instead of "dissing" them.

The response from academia was equally caustic. James Svara rejected the idea of restricting government functions to minimal core functions, saying this view implicitly maintains that "citizens should not choose programs and services for themselves that go beyond what [Eggers' and O'Leary's] definition of what is appropriate."

They offer, he declared, "a skewed, incomplete view of governmental performance to reinforce an essentially antigovernment stance," and ignore cases where governments make far reaching changes in the way they do business while maintaining responsiveness to citizens:

> "*Implicitly and explicitly, [Eggers and O'Leary] are suspicious of representative democracy because of legislators' presumed proclivity for acceding to interest groups' demands. By looking to strong elected executives as the only source of change, they ignore most of the council-manager cities (and counties) that have established positive records of accomplishment.*"

Svara also challenges the view that radical devolution will bring government closer to the public and is therefore more democratic, pointing out that "conservative forces are better able to shape policy making at the state and local levels and to weaken administrative safeguards," and that "competing state and local governments find it difficult to maintain redistributive social programs when another jurisdiction undercuts their level of service and cost."[92]

Yet there was recognition on the part of the critics that they were not engaging effectively enough with the right in the ideological battle over the role of government. "We need to articulate a case linking public administration to the public interest," Svara wrote, "that is philosophically rooted in the democratic tradition and empirically grounded in the complexities of governance and management."

Larry D. Terry, a prominent academic supporter of the reinventing government school, felt the need to urge his colleague that they "must not lose sight of the fact that ideas matter; they do have consequences."[93]

The message linking the role of government to the public interest was not being heard over the anti-government clamor that conservative think tanks were sending out through the media and drilling into their political networks and increasingly into government itself.

The Corporate Outsourcing of the Role of Government Debate

The new cohort of conservative politicians taking power in the cities, statehouses and city halls, about whom Eggers and O'Leary had written so enthusiastically, returned the favor in the mid to late 1990s by connecting more directly to the counterintelligentsia and the think tanks that supported them. This brought the latter and their "specific, arguable alternatives," which many beleaguered and staff-short state legislators were ill equipped to analyze and assess critically, closer to executive power centers and into the heart of the policymaking process.

Tommy Thompson worked closely with the Bradley Foundation and the Hudson Institute to bring welfare reform and school vouchers into government,[94] Rudolph Giuliani and Bret Schundler with the Manhattan Institute on vouchers and other issues, and a host of conservative governors and state lawmakers developed policy and legislative initiatives in every field in conjunction with the State Policy Network and American Legislative Exchange Council.

This new crop of conservative politicians included the new governor of Texas, George W. Bush, for whom Eggers went to work as project director of the Texas Performance Review, as Commissioner for the Texas Incentive and Productivity Commission, and as a designee on the Texas Council on Competitive Government. He then chaired a Government Reform Policy Committee for Bush during his first presidential campaign before moving on to serve on the OMB's Performance Measurement Advisory Commission when Bush came to power.

The privatization movement has also effectively mainstreamed itself into the lucrative world of corporate public administration consulting. A decade ago Ted Gaebler commented that a favored dubious solution for improving government was "to bring in the Big Six, to bring in the Coopers & Lybrands and the Peat Marwicks and the Arthur D. Littles and the Arthur Andersens and all the other Arthurs, to study government. I'd be embarrassed, to tell you how many millions of tax payers' dollars I personally have wasted on studies."

While some of their the names have changed, the role of these big consulting firms in producing expensive evaluations and reports for beleaguered public administrators, and in managing outsourcing for them, has grown tremendously over the past decades, as has their influence on how the debate on the proper role of government is framed.

The force of the privatization and "reinvention" waves over the past decade has created a booming market (as the libertarians might call it) for restructuring and outsourcing expertise that this industry seems eager to exploit. With the global spread of neoliberal policies, this movement has become international as well. In 1999, a Global Forum on Reinventing Government was launched in Washington, DC, hosted by Vice President Gore and co-sponsored by, among others, the World Bank, Brookings, and Stephen Goldsmith's Innovations in American Government program at Harvard. There have since been five more, and a seventh conference is schedule for June 2007 in Vienna, now being held under UN auspices.

Since 1997 a series of Outsourcing World Summits have been held, co-sponsored by Michael F. Corbett and Associates (an outsourcing consulting firm) and PricewaterhouseCoopers LLP. At the 2002 summit, the executive director of the Reason Public Policy Institute, Adrian Moore, was presented with the "World Outsourcing Award." And in early 2005, an International Association of Outsourcing Professionals (IAOP), headed by Corbett, was established by the outsourcing industry, which has dozens of corporate memberships from Fortune 500 companies and now a "Government and Nonprofit" section.[95] Privatization is a big business.

In a sense William Eggers' career tracks the progress of the privatization movement from think tank ideological hobby horse to management consultant "best practice" over the past three decades. Eggers has progressed from ardent advocate of "shock therapy" for Eastern Europe in the early 1990s, through the think tanks (Heritage, Reason and the Manhattan Institute), through a political apprenticeship with conservative administrations (in Austin and Washington, DC), to where the real action of the government restructuring industry, as Gaebler reminds us, had long been—the big public administration consulting firms.

While keeping a foot firmly planted in the conservative think tank world (as a senior fellow at the Manhattan Institute) Eggers is now "Global Director for Deloitte Research-Public Sector, where he is responsible for research and thought leadership for Deloitte's public-sector practice."[96] Apparently ever adaptable to market circumstances, this diehard opponent of "reinventing government" is now introduced on the Manhattan Institute website as an expert on "how technology can be used to reinvent government structures for greater efficiency."[97]

A key question is, where does democratic public debate about the kind of government people want fit into the nexus of strong executive downsizers and mega-consulting firms?

Network Warfare Comes to Government

The right has also achieved important breakthroughs in James Piereson's mainstreaming strategy for "getting these ideas ensconced in liberal places" such as Brookings and Harvard. In 2004, Brookings published *Governing by Network* by Goldsmith, now a professor at the Kennedy School at Harvard, and Eggers.

In this book Goldsmith and Eggers, pronouncing the privatization debate "stale," have simply changed the vocabulary and moved on to implementation. They urge public administrators not to engage in nasty frontal battles over privatization, but to work toward co-opting and neutralizing opponents of the privatization agenda. There is now an extensive accessible literature on such strategy and tactics, e.g. the Reason foundation's "How to Navigate the Politics of Privatization."

Governing by Network is a how-to book that offers strategic and tactical advice to government administrators on "the more important question of how to *manage* a government that does less and less itself."[98] Of course they dare not call this "contractor government" but find a useful euphemism, "third party government." Outside contractors provide the key force, together with the inside executive reformer, for transforming government into an administrative branch of business.

Goldsmith and Eggers depict this as part of the natural order of progression for government, involving the shrinkage of the government workforce and a massive increase in contractor revenues:[99]

> *"Federal contractors outnumbered federal employees by more than two to one and contract-generated federal jobs soared by more than 700,000 between 1999 and 2002. During the same period, the number of civil service employees actually fell by 50,000. In fact, the federal government now spends about $100 billion more annually for contracts than it does for employee salaries."*

They point to similar shifts at the state and local level, citing figures indicating that contracts to private firms "rose 65% between 1996 and 2001, reaching a total of $400 billion."

But, as they once faulted the Clinton-era reformers for not doing, they don't look at what this has meant for what government does or how well it does it. Goldsmith and Eggers praise the massive increase in prison and military contracting (which, they tell us, has enabled the military "to enhance its core war-making function") and in for-profit companies managing public schools such as Edison Project, while passing over or leaving these programs' well publicized failures unmentioned.

The concept underlying this approach is a "new governance model" that relies "less on public employees in traditional roles and more on a web of partnerships, contracts and alliances to do the public's work." Yesterday's public servant must become, Goldsmith and Eggers essentially argue, a hi-tech, bottom-line driven, e-savvy contract manager in a downsizing enterprise.

At the same time, these erstwhile proponents of "radical devolution" endorse top-down decision-making to force through competitive sourcing. In a report he wrote for ALEC and the Manhattan Institute, Eggers points to the Texas Council on Competitive Government (CCG), which he worked on for Bush, as a model because it "can compel state agencies to open functions to competition. CCG projects are also exempt from state procurement laws, a provision that helps to ensure freedom to pursue creative solutions."[100]

The workforce is to be shifted to private contractors in all areas not deemed to be part of government's core functions. Public sector unions are to be consigned to oblivion or marginalized through structural attrition and other "creative solutions" as the process of "institutionalizing competition" advances.

Nevertheless, we are told this is all in the interest of public employees. Using an argument similar to that used by the right to gut affirmative action programs across the country, Goldsmith and Eggers say that "when government insists that competition is off limits, it communicates to public workers that they are inferior."[101]

The strategy outlined in *Governing by Network* is directed at establishing control over who is involved with government reform and how opponents (not just unions, but also city council members, community organizations, and resistant businesses) can be marginalized.

It requires building and politically deploying network alliances with contractors and outside economic and institutional stakeholders (including the nonprofit sector, churches, etc.) to drive privatization forward and give it institutionalized momentum and a political base. As the Heritage Foundation's Stuart Butler pointed out, however, this is a conflictual process with a power objective:[102]

> "If skillfully designed, the privatization incentives can be made attractive to members of existing public-sector coalitions, encouraging them to 'jump ship' in favor of privatization. In this way the growth of a countervailing privatization movement can be at the expense of a coalition dedicated to larger government."

The vocabulary of networking, as Goldsmith and Eggers use it, is a warfare model that has become all the rage on the right. Developed originally in think tanks such as RAND, the model was spurred on by the internet-induced explosion of interest in networking and quickly migrated to military circles. It has since spread outward from the world of military strategy and counterinsurgency theory and is being applied by an ever-expanding group of conservative intellectuals to combating all system-challenging social forces.

Its seminal text is John Arquilla and David F. Ronfeldt's 2001 book, *Networks and Netwars: The Future of Terror, Crime and Militancy.* Goldsmith and Eggers cite Arquilla and Ronfeldt's most famous dictum, "it takes a network to fight a network," in their first chapter on the "new model of governance."

Jarol Manheim, a George Washington University political scientist, has applied this approach to the labor movement and corporate campaigns. In the Goldsmith-Eggers model it is being applied to accountable democratic government. The public sector is being subjected to"the death of a thousand cuts," the title of one of Jarol Manheim's books. [103]

"Bush's Excellent Adventure"

On coming to power in 2001 the Bush administration moved quickly to reverse Gore's "reinventing government" approach, particularly the partnership approach to public sector unions. The administration pressed more aggressively to drive competitive sourcing through the Federal agencies, and issued executive orders ending labor-management partnerships, barring project-wide collective bargaining agreements on federally funded public works, and requiring Federal contractors to post notices to workers of their right not to join unions.

The policy framework for the administration's privatization crusade is the 2002 President Management Agenda, which is "based on a strategic plan for federal outsourcing by Reason's former Privatization Director Bill Eggers, current Director of Government Redesign Carl DeMaio, and me," writes Reason Public Policy Institute executive director Adrian Moore.[104]

DeMaio, who has since left the Reason Foundation, now heads the Performance Institute, based in Virginia and San Diego. His private think tank has developed an extensive program, using poor performance and weak performance-monitoring as an agitational tool to drive privatization initiatives through the Federal government and down into the cities. Foundations are next. The "performance"-based ideological mainstreaming agenda is also now being driven into the nonprofit sector through the Council on Nonprofit Innovation, chaired by DeMaio and located at the same address as his Performance Institute.[105]

The President's management agenda, which Moore calls "Bush's Excellent Adventure," sets five strategic government-wide objectives: workforce reduction, promoting competitive sourcing, targeting "erroneous" benefit and assistance payments to Federal employees, expanding electronic government and integrating performance measures and budgeting decisions. It also promotes reliance on "faith-based initiatives" and rollbacks of civil service rights.

The administration has also driven deregulation initiatives through the departments and agencies concerned with energy and the environment, and appointed leading figures from the think tank privatization movement to oversight positions. For example, Lynn Scarlett, the former president of the Reason Foundation, is now deputy secretary of the interior and coordinates the department's environmental policy initiatives on conservation and recreation fees.

Scarlett also serves on the Executive Committee of the President's Management Council (PMC), which oversees compliance with White House management policies. According to Public Employees for Environmental Responsibility, the PMC has introduced political screening for all park service managers in the U.S. Parks Service, selecting candidates according to their loyalty to the president's management agenda.[106]

The networking arrow doesn't only move from the think tanks into government. Lori Roman, new head of the American Legislative Exchange Council's State Legislator Group, formerly headed the Office of Faith Based Initiatives in the education department where she was, as her ALEC bio puts it, "responsible for strategic planning and management of resources to achieve the goals set forth in President Bush's Management Agenda."

The Bush administration is also pressing aggressively for implementation of the 2003 Services Acquisition Reform Act (SARA) through the Office of Management and Budget's Office of Federal Procurement Policy, which was headed until last year by David Safavian, who was convicted of hiding details of his relationship with disgraced lobbyist Jack Abramoff. OMB's current "program performance" czar, Deputy Director Clay Johnson III, was Bush's chief of staff when he was governor of Texas, and was executive director of the Bush-Cheney transition.

The administration understands the importance of the wider public debate on the role of government. Under the direction of Johnson and his boss, director Rob Portman, OMB has weighed in to try and influence public perceptions by highlighting what it considers to be government program horror stories. OMB recently launched a website, Expectmore.gov, which rates government programs by effectiveness. Not surprisingly, many of the programs rated ineffective involve education, social services and economic adjustment initiatives that the administration opposes. These include

- The Education Department's Perkins loan program for needy students and its vocational education state grants;
- The Energy Department's natural gas and oil technology projects;

- The Health and Human Services Department's program to develop strategies for providing uninsured persons with health coverage; and
- The Labor Department's community service employment program for older Americans; its trade adjustment assistance program; and its program to help economically disadvantaged migrant workers achieve stable employment and economic stability.

The administration has also proposed contracting out debt collection services for the Internal Revenue Service, with the backing of the right wing National Taxpayers Union. IRS officials have acknowledged the plan will be more expensive than hiring more staff to perform the work internally, but Congress refused to appropriate funding to pay for it.

The *New York Times* reported that the government would net $1.1 billion from outsourcing collection, as opposed to some $87 billion it would collect if it the program was kept in house.[107]

Nevertheless, besides the Iraq and Katrina contracting scandals, the Bush administration's privatization efforts in the federal government have not attracted much political attention. A major looming privatization issue is a protracted battle for public assets. Working together with the Republican-controlled Congress, the Bush administration has moved to foster what is perhaps the biggest corporate grab for public assets in recent history, the privatization of government highways and roads.

This initiative has been spearheaded by both right wing think tanks such as the Reason Foundation and by major financial houses such as Goldman Sachs, which has opened discussions with more than thirty five states to promote a multibillion dollar road privatization drive.

In 2005 the administration backed a provision in the pork-laden $300 billion Federal highway bill to remove legal barriers to charging tolls on interstate highways and to grant tax free bonds to private contractors to purchase public roads. Mitch Daniels, former CEO of the Hudson Institute, Bush's ex- budget director, a recipient of Grover Norquist's "Hero of the Taxpayer" award in 2002 and now governor of Indiana, has led the charge on asset fire sales by pushing a bill through the

Indiana state legislature leasing its toll road system for seventy-five years to an Australian-Spanish consortium for $3.8 billion.

Similar deals have been cut in Michigan, Virginia, California and Chicago, which privatized the Chicago Skyway to the same consortium, Macquarie/Cintra, for $1.8 billion. In the 1980s, a $120 million privatization venture in Orange County, California came to grief when growth overtook the terms of the contract and the county had to buy back the road for $207.5 million.

Privatization: Mugged by Reality

Irving Kristol, one the main architects the intellectual assault on the role of government, once famously quipped that a neoconservative "is a liberal mugged by reality." With the intensified introduction of privatization policies in the Federal, state and local government over the past two decades, there is now a growing empirical track record for the public to judge the claims made by the think tanks and politicians that have promoted them.[108]

The horror stories about profit-motivated companies taking over government services are mounting up across the country and receiving wide, if local, media attention. In Texas, where William Eggers worked hard to promote contracting out during Bush's term as governor, the disasters have come thick and fast.

The state's decision in 2005 to replace public employees with a private contractor to screen applications for Medicare, income maintenance, long-term care and the Children's Health Insurance Program (CHIP) has turned into a fiasco. The state has had to step back in and process new applicants to allow Accenture, the company that took over the process, to catch up with its backlog. Accenture's contract fee has been cut by $50 million for work not completed.[109] Problems have also plagued the privatized Texas prison system run by the GEO Group (formerly Wackenhut), which operates 53 facilities around the country.

In Florida, comparable problems have cropped up in a $350 million contract with the Cincinnati-based Convergys Corporation to consolidate social service programs, which the *Palm Beach Post* called a "privatization disaster." Similar issues have plagued Florida's privatized state prison system, which has experienced a wave of contracting scandals involving corruption, overpayment, theft and poor services.

The GEO Group and Corrections Corporation of America (CCA), which run Florida's prisons, have both supported the American Legislative Exchange Council's efforts to promote privatization around the country.[110]

In Indiana, Daniels himself had to step in and halt the process of selecting an outside contractor to run the state's social services programs. This was to counter accusations that the head of the state's Health and Human Services department was giving preferential treatment in the bidding to an IBM-led group of companies including his former employer, Dallas-based Affiliated Computer Systems.

IV.   What Future for the Role of Government Debate?

With the headlines mounting up, the question arises whether the national "learning moment" on the role of government stimulated by social security privatization, healthcare costs, pension bailouts, Katrina, the Iraq contracting scandals and the state of the economy can be linked up with the similar "learning moments" popping up around in statehouses and cities across the country.

This is not the place to take on a discussion of public attitudes toward government or of how to shift people's core beliefs. But there is sufficient polling and research out there to suggest that an opening does exist for restoring public support for the role of government if approached in a carefully considered and comprehensive way. The ideas of collective problem solving and mutual responsibility remain strong despite decades of bipartisan initiatives focusing mainly on the rhetoric of efficiency and running government like a business.

In a report commissioned by the Frameworks Institute, the Demos Center for the Public Sector and the Council for Excellence in Government, several key findings stand out in this regard:[111]

- Americans have conflicting views of the proper role of government in society. Though they are concerned about government's capabilities, people are unwilling to give up on it. They support some reform and believe it is possible to improve public life. These perceptions of government are malleable; the public provides both positive and negative evaluations.

- The question is not whether people trust government or whether they want to expand the role of government. Sometimes they do, and sometimes they don't. Reminding people of specific government programs and services improves their view of government's effect on people's lives.

- The public recognizes that government and its programs are important to the average citizen, and believe they have benefited from public programs. They want government to provide equal opportunity, and also desire a government that will address poverty, work for a good standard of living for all, and provide a strong social safety net.

- Opinion is generally split between people who prefer "a smaller government providing fewer services" (45%) and "a bigger government providing more services" (42%). What bothers people most about taxes is the view that some are not paying their fair share. When the public considers what it dislikes about government, waste is among the most frequently mentioned issues.

- The public wants more civic engagement with government. They feel that citizens can have a positive impact on government if they get involved, and say they are prepared to participate in community, government, and politics, and significant numbers already participate. Increasing voter participation tops the list of reforms they think are necessary.

- The youngest respondents, aged 15 to 25 years old, were much stronger supporters of using government to solve problems (64%). This view declines as people age, with just 38% of those 57 years old or older supporting government problem solving.

Common Sense

William Grieder has suggested that the reigning economic ideology, developed a generation ago by Milton Friedman and Friedrich von Hayek, is now so discredited that the way is clear for new ideas. Is the way also clear for a deep shift in the way Americans view the role of government? What would a long term strategy to ignite, network and sustain such a transformative project look like?

Even if Grieder is correct that the way is clear for new economic ideas to take hold in the U.S., as we have seen the worldview of Hayek and Friedman did not achieve dominance simply because of its superior explanatory power. In fact even Friedman has acknowledged the limitations of his monetarist approach and grudgingly moved toward supply side economics.

Keynesianism did not just collapse because it failed to provide answers to the structural shifts in global capital accumulation or the fiscal crisis of the state in the 1970s. It was actively attacked and displaced by an infrastructure and a "counterintelligentsia" specifically created for that purpose because it provided the "wrong" answers (full employment and a rising standard of living financed through progressive taxation).

New Deal solutions had lost the support of a corporate and financial establishment bent on solving the country's problems through a massive slash in the social wage at a time when the base constituencies for these programs were politically too weak to respond effectively.[112] The logical alternative that presented itself, a globalized Keynesianism, was not where William Simon's colleagues in the bond market were going.[113]

All of this was made possible, as Samuel Huntington suggested thirty years ago, because the social movements that had given the welfare state its second wind (i.e., Johnson's Great Society and its "maximum feasible participation" aftermath) were waning. Whether they did so for the age-demographic reasons he cites or for other reasons is an interesting question. But wane they did. The structural decline of the labor movement and the savage attacks launched against it during this decline deepened the process.

Nevertheless, this deep shift did not reflect public opinion. As Noam Chomsky points out, polls showed that voters hoped that Reagan's legislative program would be defeated:[114]

> "The public favored tax increases devoted to New Deal and Great Society programs. Support for equal or greater social expenditures was about 80% in 1980, and increased in 1984. Cuts in Social Security were opposed with near unanimity, cuts in Medicare or Medicaid by well over 3 to 1."

Support for wide-ranging government intervention remains strong, far stronger than either centrist or right wing think tanks allow in their proposals for government reform or downsizing, which reflects the neoliberal consensus.

Over two-thirds of Americans support government guaranteed healthcare and regard this as more important than lowering taxes.

Similar levels of support for exist for aid to education and social security. As Chomsky remarks, "one can only imagine what the figures would be if the topics were not virtually off the public agenda."[115]

Neoliberal ideas became politically dominant because they received, as Powell and Simon had advocated, the backing of major corporations and the conservative foundations. They created the harder line political structures, public relations operations, communications capacities, and innovative organizing campaigns that made inroads into the thinking and voting behavior of the middle and working classes.

Their strategies ranged from crude (coded racial appeals to the white middle class in the welfare reform debates) to subtle (playing the "consumerist card"[116] in role of government debates). This enabled all of the elements of the right's networks, however disparate—from the conservative and libertarian intelligentsia to the populist anti-tax movement to the evangelical renewal movement—to turn resentment of government into "common sense." A Demos report picks up on this:[117]

> *"Another troubling focus group experience was that government is seen as a widely-shared joke, where even introducing the topic of the focus group—government—often resulted in laughter."*

Once this shift toward neoliberal hegemony and more negative public attitudes toward government deepened, not only did the ground of conservatism move to the right, but so did the strategy of triangulation pursued by many liberals and moderates. There are still strong New Democrat advocates for this strategy who believe that the "reinventing government" frame "had some fundamental long term impact on public attitudes, even though they failed to help Al Gore—the designated leader for government reinvention—in the 2000 election."[118]

But as James Mann wrote a decade ago, such technocratic and apolitical approaches to redefining the role of government will go nowhere. This process will involve reengaging the public in new ways and "politics of the highest order," including:[119]

Clashing public philosophies, battles over identities, values, and interests, and plebiscitary pressures on traditional instruments of democratic deliberation. A citizenry turned off by current modes of political expression will have to be reenergized by new social movements and reengaged in a meaningful public conversation"

Doing so means moving onto territory currently occupied largely by the right, and understanding how they have succeeded over the past three decades in downsizing democratic government.

V. Changing the Role of Government: Lessons from the Right

At the risk of oversimplification, following are some lessons that might be distilled from the right's campaigns against government:

- **Think in strategic terms. "Our job as conservatives is to wake up every day and say how do we make more of us and fewer of them"—Grover Norquist.**[cxx]

- **Don't be afraid to talk about government**. Frame it to fit your message. Avoiding it with euphemisms or just dwelling on programs won't work.

- **Politicians Never Lead**. Change positions need to be developed by outsiders, whether governing from the center right or from the base. An independent movement that targets and co-opts some of the opposition's base wins in the middle.

- **With extremely rare exceptions, the philanthropic "third sector" won't lead either.** Bring your politics (Philanthropy Roundtable, the successor organization to Kristol') and your organizational agenda (Council on Nonprofit Innovation) into the philanthropic world. Play a long game.

- **Specific arguable alternatives and concrete policies are essential.** Philosophical or ethical arguments, while indispensable, will not by themselves make change permanent. Policy planning must be in an advanced stage before "regime change" takes place, and links to politicians and their staffs must take place before coming to power (e.g., as in the Heritage Foundation's *Mandates for Leadership*).

- **You need a cluster of outsider think tanks as well as triangulating think tanks to succeed.**

- **Use the states as laboratories for mainstreaming fundamental change.** Put together a network of "change agent" politicians, and give them the backup to move out on fringe positions.

- **Populism Works** (Wallace, Reagan and Bush II). A movement can create a collective identity that becomes a source of individual identity. The right's populism is based on race, nation, religion and individual pride.

- **You can't make major change without a political and ideological base.** Facts and statistics are not what builds a base or defeats the opposition.

- **Use the power of individualism.** Individualism works: Americans are Janus-faced about government and self-reliance.

- **Optimism works** (Reagan).

- **Attack the opposition for how it governs, but don't do it using their talking points.** Language matters.

- **A movement can take on major frames and policies that are deeply embedded in the culture and overturn them (**New Deal). Age cohorts dying off helps. Norquist says this a lot. But it **must put something emotionally resonant in its place**, preferably by a crusading and charismatic leader (Reagan, Bryant, and Roosevelt). Leaders are important.

- **Freedom arguments work to pull people in.**

- **The language of reform ("reinvention") is tactically indispensable.**

- **Cooptation is a strategy to neutralize the opposition and break up its coalitions, not an ideological objective, a measure of structural change, or a defining feature of power.**

- **Negative campaigning works in policy too.** Hegemonic policy positions, even when hard wired through think tanks and in the elite, can be overturned.

- **Critical theory matters.** The Hayek school and its progeny, the public choice movement and the law and economics movement, sustained the ideological attack through five generations, largely by relentlessly confronting the dominant paradigm with high quality work. Intellectual politics matters, and the space needs to be created for this, but it must not be confused with policymaking, is not tied to the spin cycle, and is not party-driven.

- **Philosophy matters.** Think tanks that work on philosophical issues, such as the Claremont Institute and Ethics and Public Policy Center, help provide the glue for a counterintelligentsia. But this is *not framing*, it is discursive, theoretically informed, intellectually engaged and socially comprehensive.

- **Public participation in government matters: It's a threat to the right.** The attack on "maximum feasible participation" was a core strategy. Participation became dangerous at local level and at national level. Privatizing government is the way the right moved its agenda forward.

- **Politicize the business community.** Change its culture.

- **Books matter.** Under Michael Joyce's direction, the Bradley Foundation published over four hundred books. "It is what we are most proud of, of all the things we've done here," Joyce said. People may not read them, but they get reviewed, talked about etc.

- **Crack Open the opposition's consensus.** Stuart Butler of Heritage suggests proposing privatizing alternatives that divide liberal constituencies.

- **It takes a network to fight a network. A network *is not a coalition*.** A coalition is generally a collection of groups, such as an industry association or the alliance of institutions to protect civil liberties. Top down letterhead coalitions and centralized ideological vetting don't work (Norquist). A network, by contrast, refers to nodal points within and across formal and informal organizations, inside and outside government structures ("third party government").

Notes

---

[1] A year before Hurricane Katrina, Congressional leaders were warned that outsourcing was eroding FEMA's capacity to respond to disasters because its professional staff was "being systematically replaced by politically connected novices and contractors who have now 'burrowed in' to civil service jobs." Griff Witte and Charles R. Babcock, "A Major Test for FEMA and Its Contracting Crew: Sheer Scale of Katrina Awards a Concern," *Washington Post*, September 13, 2005.

[2] Steven Hill, "What's the Proper Role Of Government? Lesson From Katrina: Smaller Is Not Better," *Los Angeles Daily News*, September 25, 2005.

[3] On the price spike see McCullough Research fact sheet, at http://www.mresearch.com/pdfs/18.pdf.

[4] Bruce Bartlett, a former Heritage Foundation senior fellow (1985-87), congressional aide to Jack Kemp and an important supply side economist in the Reagan and Bush I administrations, was fired from his position with the Dallas-based National Center for Policy Analysis for daring to criticize the George W. Bush administration for its dismal record on fiscal and economic management. See Richard W. Stevenson, "In Sign of Conservative Split, a Commentator Is Dismissed," *New York Times*, October 18, 2005. Bruce Bartlett, *Impostor: How George W. Bush Bankrupted America and Betrayed the Reagan Legacy* (New York: Doubleday, 2006).

[5] "Colorado Business Leaders Warn Against Maine TABOR," Associated Press, July 28, 2006.

[6] In March 2006 the Pew Research Center noted the sharp rise (from 27% in May 2003 to 48% in March 2006) in the number of people defining President Bush as incompetent and tied this to his low approval ratings.

[7] Alan Wolfe, "Why Conservatives Can't Govern," *Washington Monthly*, July/August 2006.

[8] Dean Baker, "The Savings from an Efficient Medicare Prescription Drug Plan," Center for Economic and Policy Research, January 2006.

[9] Ann McFeatters, "Malaise Makes A Comeback: From Beirut To Big Dig, Woe Is Us," *Boston Globe*, July 29, 2006; Lisa Girion, "'Stagflation' Worries Are Mounting: New Data and a Possible Rate Hike Stir Fears of Prices Rising Amid a Languishing Economy," *Los Angeles Times*, June 15, 2006. "The real fear of the market isn't necessarily inflation, it's stagflation, a slowdown with inflationary pressures," according to one prominent stock trader. Scott Patterson, "Jobs Report Spooks Stocks," *Wall Street Journal*, July 7, 2006. Stagflation was even for a time the latest fad on Google Trends.

[10] Michael M. Phillips, "U.S. Net Debt Increases 14% To Record-Level $2.69 Trillion," *Wall Street Journal*, June 30, 2006.

[11] Jeff Bater, "U.S. Trade Deficit Widens 0.8%, Less Than Expected, on Oil Prices," *Wall Street Journal*, July 12, 2006.

[12] Steven Malanga, *The New New Left: How American Politics Works Today—Tax Eaters vs. Taxpayers* (Chicago: Ivan R. Dee, 2005). Malanga, a former editor executive editor of *Crain's New York Business*, is a contributing editor of the Manhattan Institute's City Journal, the leading journal of neoconservative urban policy.

[13] Jared Bernstein, *All Together Now: Common Sense for a Fair Economy* (San Francisco: Berrett-Koehler Publishers, 2006), pp. 84-87.

[14] The idea that the increased availability of money for investment achieved by tax cuts for corporations and those in higher income brackets will increase production, economic activity, government revenues and income.

[15] William Greider, "The Future Is Now," *The Nation*, June 26, 2006.

[16] See Thomas I. Palley, "From Keynesianism to Neoliberalism: Shifting Paradigms in Economics," in Deborah Johnston and Alfredo Saad-Filho, eds., Neoliberalism--A Critical Reader (London: Pluto Press, 2004); Palley, *Plenty of Nothing: The Downsizing of the American Dream and the Case for Structural Keynesianism* (Princeton: Princeton University Press, 1998); and Doug Henwood, *Wall Street* (New York: Verso, 1997), p. 13. According to Henwood, "free market ideology to the contrary, the role of government debt in the development of finance cannot be exaggerated."

[17] For a flavor of the issues involved see William Grieder's interview of former Clinton Treasury Secretary Robert Rubin. *The Nation* website, July 14, 2006, at www.thenation.com/doc/20060731/greiderweb.

[18] Pollster John Zogby finds that whereas 85% of frequent Wal-Mart shoppers supported Bush in the 2004 elections, they gave Bush a 35% rating in June 2006 polling. Ryan Sager, "Revenge of the Wal-Mart Voters," at www.realclearpolitics.com/articles/2006/06/revenge_of_the_walmart_voters.html.

[19] Jeff Faux, *The Global Class War: How America's Bipartisan Elite Lost Our Future—and What It Will Take to Win it Back* (New York: John Wiley, 2006), p. 231, citing June 2003 Pew poll numbers.

[20] Meg Bostrom, *"By, or for, the People? A Meta-analysis of Public Opinion of Government,"* at www.demos.org/pubs/ByOrForthePeople20050426.pdf, p. 15 and passim.

[21] Michael Lipsky and Dianne Stewart, "The Common Good Depends on Government," *Chronicle of Philanthropy*, February 23, 2006.

[22] William Greider, "The Future Is Now," *The Nation*, June 26, 2006.

[23] Lee Cokorinos, *Target San Diego: The Right Wing Assault on Urban Democracy and Smart Government* (San Diego: Center on Policy Initiatives, 2005), pp. 39-47.

[24] See Greg LeRoy, *The Great American JobsScam: Corporate Tax Dodging and the Myth of Job Creation* (San Francisco: Berrett-Koehler Publishers, 2005); and Si Kahn and Elizabeth Minnich, *The Fox in the Henhouse: How Privatization Threatens Democracy* (San Francisco: Berrett-Koehler Publishers, 2005).

[25] Grover Norquist, "Cutting the Government in Half: Three Reforms," in Reason Foundation, *Annual Privatization Report 2006: 20th Anniversary Edition*, at www.reason.org/apr2006/.

[26] Eric Foner, *Reconstruction: America's Unfinished Revolution* (New York: Harper & Row, 1988), p. 526.

[27] Eric Foner, *The Story of American Freedom* (New York: W.W. Norton, 1998), p. 121.

[28] James A. Smith, *The Idea Brokers: Think Tanks and the Rise of the New Policy Elite* (New York: Free Press, 1991), p. xv.

[29] Richard S. Tedlow, "The National Association of Manufacturers and Public Relations During the New Deal," *Business History Review*, Vol. 50, No. 1 (Spring 1976), p. 28

[30] Andrew Workman, "Manufacturing Power: The Organizational Revival of the NAM, 1941-1945," *Business History Review* 72 (Summer 1998), p. 292.

[31] Paul Samuelson's *Economics*, the Keynesian text that generations of American college students were raised on, was first published in 1948.

[32] These included the Civil Rights Act of 1964, the Economic Opportunity Act of 1964, the Elementary and Secondary Education Act of 1965, the Social Security Act of 1965 (authorizing Medicare), the National Foundation on the Arts and Humanities Act, a slew of transportation initiatives including the Highway Safety Act of 1966, and a range of environmental acts including the Wilderness Act and the Clear Air, Water Quality and Clean Water Restoration Acts.

[33] "The Road to Serfdom in Cartoons," at www.mises.org/TRTS.htm.

[34] The Planning, Programming and Budgeting System (PPBS), a systems analysis

approach to improving administration that originated with Robert McNamara in the Pentagon.

[35] On LBJ and trucking industry deregulation see the September 22, 1965 decision memorandum on transportation by Joseph Califano approved by LBJ, available here. Fannie Mae was privatized (became a government supported private entity) in 1968.

[36] The range of subjects covered on Buckley's program over the decades is remarkable. For a list see hoohila.stanford.edu/firingline/programList.php.

[37] Robert Steinback, "Reviving Faith in Role of Government," *Miami Herald*, November 9, 2005.

[38] Frances Fox Piven and Richard A. Cloward, *Regulating the Poor: The Functions of Public Welfare* (New York: Vintage Books, 2003 updated edition), p. 218.

[39] Peter Steinfels, *The Neoconservatives* (New York: Simon and Schuster, 1979), p. 9.

[40] Daniel Patrick Moynihan's 1969 polemic, *Maximum Feasible Misunderstanding: Community Action in the War on Poverty*, is the key text in this attack.

[41] Madsen Pirie, *Book of the Fallacy: A Training Manual for Intellectual Subversives* (London: Routledge, 1985).

[42] The history of how the Adam Smith Institute and other British "free market" think tanks worked to support the rise of Thatcher and shaping of her economic policies is covered in Richard Cockett, *Thinking the Unthinkable: Think Tanks and the Economic Counter-Revolution, 1931-1983* (London, Fontana Press, 1995), pp. 189-243.

[43] For an excellent discussion of this history see Jeffrey R. Henig, "Privatization in the United States: Theory and Practice," *Political Science Quarterly* (Vol. 104, No. 4, 1989-90).

[44] Henig, p. 658.

[45] Samuel P. Huntington, "The United States," in Michel J. Crozier et al., *The Crisis of Democracy* (New York: Trilateral Commission/ NYU Press, 1975), pp. 64, 73-74, 99, 107.

[46] Ibid, p. 7.

[47] Ibid., p. 113.

[48] William E. Simon, *A Time for* Truth (New York: Reader's Digest Press, 1978), 113, 155, 220. Simon began his career as a municipal bond trader.

[49] Ibid, p. 238.

[50] William L. Anderson, "Rethinking Carter," October 25, 2000, Mises Institute.

[51] Jude Wanniski, "The Mundell-Laffer Hypothesis: A New View of the World Economy," *The Public Interest*, Spring 1975.

[52] The famous Coase Theorem. Ronald Coase, the Hayek of market efficiency, property rights and transaction costs, was awarded the Nobel Prize for his work in 1991.

[53] Sidney Blumenthal, *The Rise of the Counter-Establishment: From Conservative Ideology to Political Power* (New York: Times Books, 1986).

[54] For an inside view of this process, see John J. Miller's recently published history of the Olin Foundation, *A Gift of Freedom: How the John M. Olin Foundation Changed America* (San Francisco: Encounter Books, 2006).

[55] "From Quality Circles to TQM," *Government Executive* magazine, July 1, 1997, at www.govexec.com/reinvent/articles/0797fqg2.htm.

[56] Charles L. Heatherly, ed., *Mandate for Leadership: Policy Management in a Conservative Administration* (Washington: The Heritage Foundation, 1981), pp. viii.

[57] John B. Judis, *The Paradox of American Democracy* (New York: Routledge, 2000), pp. 183-85.

[58] Heatherly, *Mandate for Leadership I*, p. 700.

[59] Miller, *A Gift of Freedom*, p. 119.

[60] Ronald Brownstein and Nina Easton, *Reagan's Ruling Class* (Washington: Presidential Accountability Group, 1982), pp. 338-339.

[61] "Federal Housing Official Quits After Inquiry Cites Abuses Of Office," *The New York*

Times, July 8, 1983.

[62] Mike Davis, "Who Killed LA?" *New Left Review* 197 (January-February 1993), p. 10.

[63] E.S. Savas, *Privatization in the City: Successes, Failures, Lessons* (Washington, DC: CQ Press, 2005).

[64] Stuart M. Butler, "Changing the Political Dynamics of Government," *Proceedings of the Academy of Political Science*, Vol. 36, No. 3 (1987), p. 5.

[65] Since renamed the National Council for Public-Private Partnerships.

[66] Heritage Foundation, "Privatizing Federal Services: A Primer," February 20, 1986 at www.heritage.org/Research/Budget/upload/87528_1.pdf.

[67] Robert W. Poole, Jr. "Ronald Reagan and the Privatization Revolution," June 8, 2004, Reason.org.

[68] Madsen Pirie, *Dismantling the State: The Theory and Practice of Privatization* (Dallas, TX: National Center for Policy Analysis, 1985).

[69] Fred L. Smith, Jr., "Privatization at the Federal Level," *Proceedings of the Academy of Political Science*, (Vol. 36, No. 3, 1987), p. 186.

[70] Paul Starr, "The Limits of Privatization," in Steve Hanke, ed., *Prospects for Privatization* (New York: Academy of Political Science, 1987), reprinted in revised and expanded form by the Economic Policy Institute in 1988; and Lester M. Salamon, "Privatization: The Challenge to Public Management. Report of the National Academy of Public Administration's Panel on the Management of Privatization," March 1989.

[71] Miller, *A Gift of Freedom*, p. 127, 129. The book was *Politics, Markets, and America's Schools* by John E. Chubb and Terry M. Moe. Moe is an ardent foe of teachers unions and has advocated using charter schools and vouchers as a means of breaking their political power. Terry M. Moe, "Teachers Unions and the Public Schools," in *A Primer on America's Schools* (Palo Alto: Stanford University Press, 2001).

[72] Jeffrey R. Henig, "Privatization in the United States: Theory and Practice," *Political Science* Quarterly, (Vol. 104, No. 4, 1989-90), p. 663.

[73] *Micropolitics* (1988), *Privatisation: Theory, Practice and Choice* (1988), and *Blueprint for a Revolution* (1993), which contains the discussion of vouchers.

[74] Ibid., p. 187.

[75] Judis, *The Paradox of American Democracy*, p. 210.

[76] Council for Excellence in Government, "Attitudes Toward Government," July 1997, online at CEE website.

[77] Ibid.

[78] Available here and here.

[79] For an incisive discussion of this see Daniel W. Williams, "Reinventing the Proverbs of Government," *Public Administration Review* (Vol. 60, No. 6, Nov.-Dec. 2000).

[80] "Remarks By The President to DLC National Conversation," White House press release, June 4, 1998.

[81] Laurence E. Lynn, "Government Lite," *The American Prospect*, December 1, 1994.

[82] "Remarks by the President," op. cit.

[83] Bob Woodward, *The Agenda: Inside the Clinton White* House (New York: Pocket Books, 1994), p. 388

[84] Stuart M. Butler and Kim R. Holmes, eds., *Mandate for Leadership IV* (Washington, DC: Heritage Foundation, 1997), p. 137.

[85] Louis Jacobson, "Clinton Signs Privatization Bill," *Christian Science Monitor*, October 22, 1998.

[86] Paul C. Light, "The Right Way To Streamline Bureaucracy" *Christian Science Monitor*, September 14, 2006. According to Light, while the federal workforce remained basically steady from 1999-2002, "during the same period contract-generated jobs went up by more than 700,000 jobs and grant-generated jobs by 333,000." Paul C. Light, "The True Size of

Government," NYU Wagner School Research Organizational Performance Initiative Brief No. 2 (August 2006), p. 7.

[87] Cokorinos, *Target San Diego*, pp. 33-44.

[88] Task Force on Excellence in State and Local Government, *Working Together for Public Service*, p. 66.

[89] George Nesterczuk, "Reviewing the National Performance Review," *Regulation* (Cato Institute), Volume 19, Number 3, 1996.

[90] For more on Roe see Cokorinos, *Target San Diego*, pp. 13-17, 22.

[91] William D. Eggers and John O'Leary, *Revolution at the Roots: Making Our Government Smaller, Better and Closer to* Home (New York: Free Press, 1995), p. 328. [Cited in Svara].

[92] James H. Svara, "Reforming or Dismantling Government?" *Public Administration Review* (Vol. 56, No. 4, July 1996), p. 404.

[93] Larry D. Terry, "Administrative Leadership, Neo-Managerialism, and the Public Management Movement," *Public Administration Review* (Vol. 58, No. 3, May/June 1998), p. 198

[94] The late Michael Joyce, Bradley's longtime president, served as an informal advisor to Thompson when he became secretary of Health and Human Services in 2001 and to the White House Office on Faith Based Initiatives. On Hudson and Thompson see Mike Flaherty, "Think Tank Influencing Thompson: Group Drew Framework for New W-2 Program," *Wisconsin State Journal*, February 1, 1997, p. 1A.

[95] IAOP's website lists the following companies in the government/education category: Accenture, Aramark, Beijing Software Testing, Capgemini, CGI Group, Colorchips India, EMCOR Group, Intetics, Mastek Ltd., Shanghai Wicresoft, Sodexho Alliance and Unisys.

[96] For more on Deloitte's role in "whipsawing" states and localities in the competitive battle over "business climate," see Greg LeRoy, *The Great American JobsScam*, op. cit, pp. 69-88.

[97] William D. Eggers, Manhattan Institute bio.

[98] Stephen Goldsmith and William D. Eggers, *Governing by Network: The New Shape of the Public* Sector (Brooking Institution Press, 2004), p. 24.

[99] Ibid., 11.

[100] William D. Eggers, "Show Me the Money: Budget-Cutting Strategies for Cash-Strapped States," ALEC and Manhattan Institute, 2002.

[101] William D. Eggers and Stephen Goldsmith, "This Works: Managing City Finances," Civic Bulletin (Manhattan Institute), No. 31 March 2003.

[102] Stuart M. Butler, "Changing the Political Dynamics of Government," p. 9, emphasis in original.

[103] Manheim has written two books that have become key texts in anti-union think tank and law firm libraries, *The Death of a Thousand Cuts: Corporate Campaigns and the Attack on the Corporation*, and *Biz-War and the Out-Of-Power Elites: The Progressive-Left Attack on the Corporation*.

[104] Adrian Moore, "Bush's Excellent Adventure," *Reason Report*, Spring 2002, Issue No. 94, p. 3.

[105] On DeMaio see Cokorinos, *Target San Diego*, pp. 39-47. On the nonprofit sector, see the Council for Nonprofit Innovation (CNI) website.

[106] Public Employees for Environmental Responsibility, Press Release, October 13, 2005.

[107] David Cay Johnston, "I.R.S. Enlists Help in Collecting Delinquent Taxes," *New York Times*, August 20, 2006.

[108] For an overview see Mildred E. Warner and Amir Hefetz. "Privatization and the Market Role of Government," Economic Policy Institute, Briefing Paper, 2001; and Michael J. Ballard and Mildred E. Warner, "Taking the High Road: Local Government Restructuring and the Quest for Quality," Cornell Working Papers in Planning #194,

April 2000.

[109] Christine Vestal, "States Stumble Privatizing Social Services," Stateline.org, August 4, 2006.

[110] Sarah Posner, "Security for Sale," *American Prospect*, January 5, 2006.

[111] Meg Bostrom, "By, or for, the People? A Meta-analysis of Public Opinion of Government," Demos (New York), March 25, 2005.

[112] Stanley Aronowitz, *How Class Works: Power and Social* Movements (New Haven: Yale University Press, 2003), pp. 28, 128-129

[113] David Harvey, *A Brief History of Neoliberalism* (New York: Oxford University Press, 2005), Chapter 2.

[114] Noam Chomsky, *Failed States: The Abuse of Power and the Assault on* Democracy, (New York: Metropolitan Books, 2006), p. 215.

[115] Ibid., citing extensive polling in Chicago Council on Foreign Relations, *Global Views 2004* (Chicago: CCFA, 2004), pp. 14-15.

[116] "How to Talk About Government: A Frameworks Message Memo," FrameWorks Institute, 10

[117] Marcia Kinsey and Patrick Bresette, "A Focus on Government: Key Findings From Focus Groups," Demos Center for the Public Sector, *Public Briefing No. 4* (October 2005).

[118] William A. Galston and Elaine C. Kamarck, "The Politics of Polarization," Third Way (Washington, DC), October 2005, p. 15.

[119] Thomas E. Mann, "Is the Era of Big Government Over?" *Public Perspective* (Brookings), February-March 1998.

[120] "The World according to Grover," *American Prospect* website, July 6, 2006.